RAPID TRAINING

OF A

COMPANY FOR WAR

RAPID TRAINING of a COMPANY for WAR

By

CAPTAIN A. P. BIRCHALL

Royal Fusiliers

Instructional Staff, Western Canada, 1913-14

2nd EDITION.

The Naval & Military Press Ltd

Published by

The Naval & Military Press Ltd

Unit 5 Riverside, Brambleside
Bellbrook Industrial Estate
Uckfield, East Sussex
TN22 1QQ England

Tel: +44 (0)1825 749494

www.naval-military-press.com
www.nmarchive.com

PREFACE

The writer being debarred by ill-health from taking an active part during the first three months of the war, has taken the opportunity of putting on paper the fruits of many years' experience of company training.

The main object of the following pages is to assist the Company Officers and Non-Commissioned Officers of the New Armies, the Oversea Forces, and the Territorial Force in training their companies for service in the present war.

It is realised that the training of the above forces must be carried out as efficiently as possible in the very short time available.

The writer has no intention whatever of supplanting the official textbooks; there is nothing which can take the place of their study.

But it is not always easy for Officers who have had little experience to apply the lessons taught in these books. It is hoped that inasmuch as the following pages are the result of much practical company experience, followed by the useful experience of an instructor, they may be found of some help to Company Officers and Non-Commissioned Officers in the direction indicated.

Where possible, incidents in the present war have been drawn attention to in order to illustrate valuable lessons.

In the Appendix a chapter has been added on the subject of "Lice in War," which, though it cannot strictly be included under the heading of "Company Training," may be found useful, it is hoped, by all proceeding to the front.

A reference card has been inserted at the end of the book containing important details of information for the benefit of Company Officers and Non-Commissioned Officers.

It is thought that by having this card in his pocket to refer to, the Officer or Non-Commissioned Officer will have with him a useful aid to his memory.

The chapters devoted to Company Training should be read in connection with "Notes on Company Training," issued by the General Staff, September, 1914.

November, 1914.

PREFACE TO 2ND EDITION.

Owing to the unexpected support accorded this small handbook, it has been found necessary to issue a second edition within a few weeks of the publication of the first.

Advantage has been taken to bring the book absolutely up to date in accordance with the most recent experiences of our troops at the front. This is especially the case in the chapter on Engineering.

In the Appendix there has also been added a short article on " Customs of the Service." Though this subject is not strictly germane to the title of the book, it is the writer's experience that many officers of the New Armies, Overseas Forces, and Territorial Force are frequently in doubt as to the custom of the service in many minor matters of military etiquette. It is hoped that this article may therefore be found of use.

January, 1915,

PREFACE TO 2ND EDITION.

Owing to the unexpected support accorded this small handbook, it has been found necessary to issue a second edition within a few weeks of the publication of the first.

Advantage has been taken to bring the book absolutely up to date in accordance with the most recent experiences of our troops at the front. This is especially the case in the chapter on Engineering.

In the Appendix there has also been added a short article on "Customs of the Service." Though this subject is not strictly germane to the title of the book, it is the writer's experience that many officers of the New Armies, Overseas Forces, and Territorial Force are frequently in doubt as to the custom of the service in many minor matters of military etiquette. It is hoped that this article may therefore be found of use.

January, 1915,

CONTENTS

CHAPTER XII.

AIRCRAFT AND INFANTRY, ETC., ETC.

APPENDICES.

DIAGRAMS.

ABBREVIATIONS.

I.T. = Infantry Training, 1914.
F.S.R., Part I. = Field Service Regulations,
   Part I., 1909 (Reprint, 1912).
M.F.E. = Manual Field Engineering, 1911.
F.S.P.B. = Field Service Pocket Book, 1913.
Musk. Regs. = Musketry Regulations, Part I.,
   1909 (Reprint, 1914).

RAPID TRAINING

OF A

COMPANY FOR WAR

CHAPTER I.

GREAT RESPONSIBILITIES.

A Word to Company Commanders—A Word to all Company Officers and N.C.O.'s—Discipline.

A WORD TO COMPANY COMMANDERS.

The responsibility of training the company for war is a great one. You may be deemed fortunate in the prospect of seeing the result of your work tested shortly after it is completed. Hitherto few have had that chance.

The main points that it is wise to take into consideration in getting the best results of your training would seem to be as follow :—

1. Shortness of time available. You can only expect a few weeks for company training.
2. The consequent need for concentration on really important matters, and elimination of non-essentials. Anything which does not tend directly to efficiency in war should be avoided.
3. A realisation that you are dealing with men who are enthusiasts, but who are for the most part utterly ignorant of the profession which they have suddenly taken up.
4. A full appreciation of the fact that your crowning difficulty will not be the training of the men, but that of the officers and N.C.O.'s.

A WORD TO ALL COMPANY OFFICERS AND N.C.O.'s.

You should realise that you are solely responsible for your command, whether that be a platoon or section. If there is anything wrong, you are the responsible man.

Make up your mind that your own command shall be the best in the regiment. It is necessary to recognise at once that the task of commanding men in peace, and still more that of leading them in war, is a very difficult one, and needs all your energy and all your ability; if it takes a private soldier seven hours a day to learn his job, it will unquestionably take you ten hours. Study the official books (confining yourself to the portions of them which you are sure will be of use to you), watch other men, who are in a similar position in other companies or in other regiments, and who obviously know their job.

If you have previous experience, do not imagine that you know all that there is to be known; military science changes rapidly, and what was all right in 1904 may be all wrong in 1914.

By these means only, will you attain to that self respect and self confidence which are absolutely essential for successful leadership. There is no more pathetic sight than a man attempting to exercise command for which he is obviously unfitted, and as a rule no one is more painfully conscious of the fact than himself.

DISCIPLINE.

As an American has aptly put it—

"A man without discipline in war is about as much use as a fan in Hell."

What does discipline, then, imply? It implies prompt and unquestioning obedience to all orders received.

No army in the history of the world has ever been successful unless its foundations have been laid in strict discipline. The basis on which the discipline rests varies in different armies. For instance, Japanese discipline is founded on religion and patriotism; German discipline is founded on fear; British discipline is founded on esprit-de-corps and mutual good feeling between ranks.

The question then is how to obtain this necessary quality of discipline.

1. (a) Avoid familiarity with the ranks below you; such familiarity unquestionably breeds contempt.

   (b) Avoid a patronising manner towards your subordinates or the use of sarcasm at their expense; it merely irritates.

   (c) Avoid any argument over an order given; hesitation to obey an order is an offence in itself, and the offender should at once be placed under arrest.

If the men under you see that you mean business they will never "try it on" with you.

(d) Avoid "telling off" any subordinate officer or non-commissioned officer in the presence of the men.

2. Do your utmost to know your job; men will always respect a leader who is up to his work.

3. Give your orders in the tone and manner that you would like to receive orders in, were you in your men's place. Probably half the offences against discipline in the Army are due to tactlessness or a bad manner on the part of Officers or Non-Commissioned Officers.

4. Set a good example; you want your men to be smart—be, therefore, smart yourself. There is no more nauseating sight than to see an Officer who is badly turned out, or has a dirty jacket, checking men in the ranks for similar lapses. An Officer cannot be too smart.

5. Study the characters of your men—let them see that their interests are your interests—in time they will come to regard you in the light of a friend.

6. Study the comfort of your men. A little care on your part will often add greatly to their comfort; when in barracks, camp, or bivouac, keep a watchful eye especially on their food; the rations are complete and should ensure every non-commissioned officer and man having at least three good meals (of which two should be meat meals) a day; if the food served appears insufficient or unappetising it is due to bad management or bad cooking; both these can be corrected. Make a point of noticing how much food is left over at the end of dinner. If you find that there is a fair amount of meat frequently left over, a corresponding amount should be cut off the meat ration for that mess before it is cooked, and this should be made use of for tea or breakfast the following day. The same with the bread. When on manœuvre always see to it that your men get their meals before you get your own.

The only satisfactory course in barracks, camp, or bivouac is for an officer of the company to visit the various messes at each meal and personally to satisfy himself that the fare provided is good and sufficient; the visit of the Orderly Officer is frequently a mere formality, and the fact that there are " no complaints " generally means little or nothing.

CHAPTER II.

RESULTS AIMED AT.

Results Desired in the Short Time Available—
Special Qualifications for Officers and Non-
Commissioned Officers—Drill.

Let the Company Commander, if given a
free hand by his Commanding Officer, decide
for himself what results he hopes to achieve
in the brief time that is available.

These may be summarised as below : —

REQUIRED OF THE COMPANY.

1. The company must be physically fit,
   able to march and fight, stand fatigue
   and endure discomfort, and in the end
   privation.
2. The company must be able to shoot, to
   judge distance, and exhibit good fire
   discipline.
3. The company must be able to skirmish,
   advance against an entrenched position, practise mutual support and reinforcing, assault the position, and carry
   out a retirement.

4. The company must be able to take its share in protective work, by day and night, either on outpost duty or as part of an advanced, rear, or flank guard on the march.

5. The company must be efficient with the spade both by day and night, and be able to put a position in a state of defence.

6. The company must be able to carry out efficiently night advances and night attacks.

7. In addition to the men who will be required as signallers and machine-gun men, and who will be trained regimentally, one non-commissioned officer and four men also must be trained as scouts, and two men as expert range takers.

In addition to above, further qualifications must be required from the officers, sergeants, and corporals.

OFFICERS', SERGEANTS', AND CORPORALS' EXTRA QUALIFICATIONS.

8. They must be able to direct and control fire, including the accurate judging of

distance, good description of targets, and control of the expenditure of ammunition.

9. They must have " an eye for ground," and be able to lead men effectively either in advance or retirement, and show initiative.

10. They must have some tactical knowledge and be quick of decision. (Indecision in any commander, from a captain to a corporal, is a serious failing.)

11. They must be able to write a concise, intelligible message or report, and the officers should be able to make a rough sketch.

12. The officers and a proportion of sergeants should be able to use the range-finder.

13. The officers and sergeants must also have a fair knowledge of map reading, and be able to make use of the sun and stars in finding their way across country by day or night. The officers should also be able to march on a compass bearing by day and night.

It will be noticed that no reference is here made to drill. The omission is intentional.

DRILL.

Drill is liable to be made a god of by non-Regular troops. An officer who is not good at his drill is often regarded as a waster, regardless of his abilities in other directions.

This idea must be got rid of at any cost, otherwise vastly more important work will be sacrificed to drill.

Drill has a very distinct place in the military art, but it must be kept to its place.

It should be regarded as a means to an end, not an end in itself.

It is best considered in this way. A recruit must start his military work with drill. It teaches him prompt, unquestioning obedience to orders—the essence of discipline.

It further teaches him a habit of working with others under a common leader; these virtues are especially the result of elementary drill.

He is then taught section, platoon, and company drill. The chief object of these is mainly to teach all ranks quick decision and quick action following it, as well as to enable each unit to take its place in the higher formation.

Therefore we say drill is essential to a recruit, and a certain amount of platoon and company drill is advisable for all trained men, but it must be strictly limited.

Directly the recruit can drill with fair proficiency, and the company can carry out company drill without frequent errors, drill should give place almost entirely to more important work. For a company in the New Armies or in the Territorial Force to endeavour to obtain Guard-like precision in drill is little short of criminal, as it can only imply the sacrifice of their work in the field.

BAYONET FIGHTING.

It may further be noticed that no reference is here made to bayonet-fighting.

The reason for this omission lies in the fact that in the five weeks' company training contemplated by the Authorities bayonet-fighting is not included.

This, presumably, would be carried on progressively before and after company training.

We will now proceed to offer suggestions as to how best to obtain the above-mentioned requirements in the matter of training.

CHAPTER III.

MARCHING AND MUSKETRY.

Physical Fitness—Marching and March Discipline — Sanitation — Musketry Efficiency—Judging Distance.

PHYSICAL FITNESS.

This includes physical development by Swedish exercises—ability to march long distances without undue fatigue—the endurance of discomfort without complaint—and the carrying out of protracted operations in the field.

It is an accepted fact that the Swedish exercises are invaluable for improving the physique and strengthening the muscles.

If it is impossible to obtain the services of a qualified instructor, and there is no possibility of getting a couple of non-commissioned officers trained as instructors, two non-commissioned officers should be specially detailed to learn the syllabus from the official books issued on the subject. This should not take long for intelligent men.

MARCHING.

This includes march discipline, care of the feet, and an ability to keep going all day.

This subject is so well, and yet briefly, dealt with in the official books (I.T., Sec. 112, and F.S.R., Part I., Secs. 24-26, 30, 31) that it is unnecessary to add much here.

As regards halts, probably the best arrangement is five minutes after the first half-hour and ten minutes in every hour afterwards. Directly the signal to halt is given the duration of the halt should be rapidly passed down from the head of the column to the rear. Every non-commissioned officer and man should at once remove his "pack."

Cigarette smoking during a march (including the halts) should be forbidden.

The great art in marching is steady progress in distance. The sure road to success is causing the men to forget that they are marching; for this purpose singing should be strongly encouraged, and a mouth-organ band (say, six or eight men who are recompensed by having their rifles carried for them on the transport) will be found very useful.

Above all, keep the pace uniform, and allow no "hurrying up" or stepping out. All distance lost (and there should be less each day) should be made up at the halts.

Every company should do its utmost to reduce " falling out " to a minimum.

The best of all ways to do this is to stimulate a pride in the company, and thus make it almost a point of honour not to fall out. When imbued with this spirit men will " stick it," though doing so may be pain and grief.

Sometimes it may be necessary in the case of a physically weak man to help him along towards the end of a trying march by relieving him of his rifle, but the practice should be a very rare one, and only to be employed in extreme cases.

WATER BOTTLES.

The water bottle should be regarded in the light of an emergency ration, to be used only when all else fails. A company will never march well if the men drink out of their water bottles whenever they feel thirsty.

In some brigades drinking from the water bottle is only allowed by special permission of the senior officer present.

CARE OF THE FEET.

One word as to care of the feet. This is all important. Each company officer and non-commissioned officer should take as much interest in the state of his men's feet as he does in their turn-out on parade, or in the state of their rifles. Foot inspections should take place after each day's march or manœuvre; it is a good idea for the non-commissioned officer accompanying the officer inspecting to have with him a supply of lint, bandage, boracic powder, and plaster. This will save many visits to the Medical Officer. The officer commanding company will do well to insist on every non-commissioned officer and man having three serviceable pairs of socks in his kit, and two well-fitting and serviceable pairs of marching boots. It will be wise, too, for the officer commanding company to arrange for the battalion chiropodist occasionally to accompany him round during a company foot inspection.

The socks should be washed, if possible, every third day and thoroughly dried.

Before a march, soaping the socks is recommended for men with tender feet; sprinkling the feet with boracic powder is also a good thing. When taken off, socks should be stretched and well shaken. Blisters should be pricked with a clean needle, and all tender parts smeared over with some simple ointment or soap.

BOOTS.

Much trouble is frequently caused by the careless fitting of boots. The officer commanding company should make it a rule that an officer is present whenever men are issued with boots. Otherwise it is frequently done in a haphazard manner, the recruit being chiefly anxious not to give trouble.

The officer superintending the issue should see the boots on, and the man walk up and down in them, to make certain that they fit; if the man has any doubt about the right size, suggest the larger of the two.

The man should always be ordered to " break them in " at once—not by using them on a route march to start with, but about barracks or camp.

INSTRUCTION IN HYGIENE.

Under this heading of physical fitness we may include instruction in hygiene and camp sanitation.

The necessity of personal cleanliness, of regular washing of underclothes, and, above all, of strict obedience to rules of sanitation in camp and bivouac must be emphasised.

MUSKETRY EFFICIENCY.

This will include (a) Marksmanship on the range and at field firing, (b) Judging distance, (c) Fire discipline.

Marksmanship.—Let your aim be " a high average of marksmanship for the company." Do not concern yourself over much with the best shots, they can be trusted to look after themselves, but *endeavour to improve the weak shots*, by finding out the cause of their failure, by carefully watching them as they fire, and testing their aim by the triangle of error method, etc. (Musk. Regs., Part I., Para. 207.)

Above all, remember that before a man is allowed on the range he should be given thorough preliminary instruction, including aiming instruction and muscle exercises, and be taught good practical firing positions. Never attempt, however, to alter a man's firing position if he has had previous experience and is a good shot. In cases where it is possible he should also be given practice on the miniature range.

Directly the recruit has been properly grounded in his musketry work and commenced his range practices every effort should be made to make him a rapid and fairly accurate shot. It has been found that our one great advantage over the Germans lies in our rapid shooting. The German is slower and less accurate.

It is only by the ability of our men to pour in a steady hail of bullets, say, 25 rounds a minute, that the German assaults, made in great masses, have been repulsed.

It is not to be supposed that this rapid rate of fire can really be aimed. But our object should be, firstly, to get the highest possible rate of aimed fire, and, secondly, an even greater rate of unaimed fire, for the reason just referred to.

To achieve this end, daily practice in rapid loading and firing, with dummy cartridges, is necessary. Ten minutes a day at this practice now will probably save a company's annihilation later on.

JUDGING DISTANCE.

This is a branch of military science that has very rarely had the attention bestowed on it, outside the Regular Army, that it

deserves. The importance of it can hardly be
exaggerated. If it is necessary for a private
to be able to judge distance, it is a hundred
times more so for the officer and non-commissioned officer. The argument, then, from this
is that the officer and non-commissioned officer
will require much training in this subject
additional to that given to the men.

The aids to correct judging distance are
well shown in Musk. Regs., Part I., Paras.
312-315.

Combined with practice in Judging Distance should be Visual Training. Long-dis-
tance eyesight and the ability to '' pick up ''
indistinct objects are obviously of great importance in the field; they can be greatly
improved by practice. The following system
of carrying out these practices is recommended.

JUDGING DISTANCE PRACTICES.

Choose some ground where objects can be
seen in different directions up to about a
mile.

Take out one officer or non-commissioned
officer and four men (all good judges of distance); the men to act as '' points '' and the
officer or non-commissioned officer to help you

place them. Select a high spot with a good view; put a stick into the ground to mark it.

Then step off the distances you have decided on, say three under 700 yards, and one between 700 and 800. Whilst you are doing two, your assistant is doing the other two in other directions; the points go out with you. On arriving at the correct distance place the man in such a way that he is only partially visible and has to be eye-searched for, either partially behind cover, or, if in the open, kneeling, or, at any range under 400, lying down. Tell him he is No. 1, 2, 3, or 4 point, and that he is, for the present, to conceal himself as far as possible, but to keep his eye on the centre point, and when he sees the signalling flag waved his number of times, he is to shew himself according to the amount decided on. If, after that signal is given, the flag is waved rapidly from side to side, that is a signal for him to make himself more conspicuous.

It is sometimes arranged for the distant points to be provided with rifles and a few rounds of blank ammunition, which they fire while they are being judged on; this gives an extra test in location by sound, but the smoke produced by the firing makes the practice easier, and is unreal.

R. T.   C

Having arranged the points you return to the centre point, carefully checking the distance by pacing; you then have a rehearsal of the practice, calling each " point " up in turn by means of your signalling flag.

Supposing the country is not sufficiently flat, or too intersected with hedges or other obstacles for accurate pacing, it will be necessary to take the ranges over 500 yards with the range finder. In any case it is advisable to take those over 700 yards, thereby saving considerable time.

Directly you have tested the " points " you are then ready for the company. You should have so arranged that they should be in the neighbourhood by the time required (obviously they must not see the testing of the points).

You then station the Company in line facing, and at right angles to the first point, with their centre resting on the centre point.

You then call out the Section Commanders, armed with judging distance registers, with the name of their non-commissioned officers and men inscribed therein, and they take up position ten paces in front of their sections facing the front. You then, from behind the company, call up the first point, having previously cautioned the company *against a*

word being spoken during the test.   You
allow 30 seconds for every man to " pick up "
the " point." You then direct anyone who
does not see him to take a pace forward—
the section commander makes immediate note
of any such men (with a view, if they fail
again to " pick up " the point, to further
practice in visual training). The object is
then pointed out to these men and they fall
back into the ranks.   The section commander
now estimates the distance and enters his
estimate on his register ; he then calls out his
section from his register.   Each man as he is
called goes quickly up to the section commander, whispers his estimate of the distance,
and proceeds a further ten paces to the front ;
when there, he is allowed to " stand easy "
and to talk.   (Arrangements must be made
for the Officers to be placed on the register
of one of their sections ; they should give their
estimate after the Section Commander has
recorded his own.)

Directly the recording is completed you call
out the correct distance ; this is entered on
the register.

The company is now marched back to the
centre point and faced in the direction of No.
2 point.   The same process is continued
until all 4 points have been judged on.

On return to quarters the mean percentage of error of each man is worked out and entered on the register (Musk. Regs., Part I, Para. 325).

JUDGING DISTANCE AS A PASTIME.

Every endeavour should be made to get the Company to look upon " judging distance " as an interesting pastime as well as a necessary accomplishment.

To this end encourage the men whenever in the country to argue among themselves the question of the distance of various objects.

Even if no steps are taken to test an estimate, the consideration of it and the different opinions expressed are useful.

A good judge of distance, who has been willing to back his opinion, has been known to make quite a sum of money in this way, and incidentally to have supplied much zest to the pastime, and much instruction to his victims!

FIRE DISCIPLINE.
(See I. T., Sec. 117.)

This is not easy to practise except at field firing; it is, however, of the greatest importance, combined with Fire Control on the part of the platoon and section leaders. (See page 112.)

CHAPTER IV.

SYSTEM OF TRAINING.

General Principles—Combination of Practice and Explanation—Lectures—Careful Preparation of Work—Explanation to the Company—Encouragement of Initiative — Regard for Men's Comfort—Wet Weather.

GENERAL PRINCIPLES.

Having now dealt with the subjects of Physical Fitness, Drill, and Musketry and its sister subjects, we now come to the actual Field Training of the Company. Here again we must confine ourselves to what is absolutely necessary as a preparation for war.

Before entering into the detail of the work a few general principles may be usefully laid down.

1. Combine all practical work with lecture and explanation.

    Always make up your mind overnight exactly what you are going to do and the lessons you want to teach. Work on a definite syllabus, which should be progressive.

3. Whatever the scheme is, or whatever the task allotted to the Company, explain it thoroughly to the Company before you start.

4. Do your utmost to encourage initiative on the part of your Officers and non-commissioned officers.

5. Have regard to the comfort of your men—do not parade them till necessary, and do not keep them standing when they could equally well be sitting or lying down.

A word or two about each of these general principles :—

1. COMBINATION OF PRACTICE AND EXPLANATION.

As a rule when the company has been inspected on the morning parade after breakfast, it is wise to explain in a few words the plan for the morning. When making these explanations do not attempt to address the company in line; it is merely foolish; nor attempt a complicated manœuvre like making a kind of hollow square. All you have to do is to shout "Gather round."

The programme having been explained, you carry it out, arranging, however, for a half-hour break in the middle of the morning (if the work is of the nature of Protection, etc., it may not be possible to arrange a break). The first quarter of an hour of the break should be devoted to a brief criticism of the work done, or to the lessons to be learnt from it, the men being seated. The last quarter should be a " rest easy " for the men ; this gives them the chance of a smoke.

LECTURES.

Besides the instruction conveyed as above, there should be definite lectures given of 30 to 40 minutes duration on the work in hand, say at least 3 days a week.

These should be carefully prepared, and, as a rule, delivered from notes (a blackboard is invaluable if obtainable); writing lectures word for word is too lengthy a business for our present object. It is well to get each Officer to help with these lectures, giving them good warning for the purpose of careful preparation ; as far as possible, consistent with the syllabus, allow them to choose their own subject.

Every endeavour should be made to render

these lectures interesting; with this object
the following hints may be found useful :—

- (1.) Illustrate a point by personal experience where possible; this should be done within reason. Some Officers with South African experience are inclined to overdo this.

- (2.) Illustrate a point by reference to a recent war where possible.

- (3.) Introduce a note of humour every now and then; a joke, even though a poor one, has been known to revive a sleepy audience.

- (4.) At the beginning of a lecture question individuals on points of the last lecture on the same subject.

- (5.) Go slow, and lay stress on the main points.

- (6.) Invite questions at the end of a lecture.

2. CAREFUL PREPARATION OF WORK BEFOREHAND.

The syllabus of work should, if possible, be made out at the beginning of the training, denoting the work to be got through

each week; a margin of time should be left.
Before the week's work starts, each day's
work should be allotted. Much thought will
be required on the part of the Company Commander the previous evening in order to
make the best use of each day's training.

3. EXPLANATION TO COMPANY OF ALL WORK IN HAND.

A few years ago it was thought that a
soldier was a machine, and should never be
allowed to think for himself; the South
African War altered all that, as far as our
Army was concerned; the soldier is now
taught to use his brains and to take advantage of ground and cover, with results which
have been amply justified during the present
war. In other words, our men are regarded
as intelligent human beings.

It follows from this that the more one
can interest them in the work in hand the
better they will do it. Take an example:—
The company is paraded and inspected. It
is then marched off; the men have no idea
whether they are going to march for hours,
or to carry out some scheme, or to operate
against another company. What interest
can they take? The march becomes tedious
and irksome.

If, on the other hand, the Officer Commanding Company tells them before they start that they are marching to a certain spot where they will act as an advanced guard to an imaginary force, and are likely to meet a " skeleton " enemy at any time, every man in the company takes an interest in what is going forward, and marches along with a light heart, entirely oblivious of the 45lbs. dead weight he is carrying.

It is a sound rule for an Officer Commanding Company, when working under battalion arrangements, directly he gets his orders, to assemble the company at once, and explain to them *all he knows;* of course, there are occasions when this may not be desirable, especially on active service, but as a general rule it will be found to act as a most useful stimulus, whilst it need only take a few minutes. Some officers prefer to explain things to their platoon commanders or section leaders, and for them to explain things in turn to their men ; it is doubtful, however, whether this is as effective, and it certainly takes twice as long, which is frequently a vital point.

Further, never omit after any manœuvre in the field to tell the company what in your opinion were the results of the manœuvre and any lessons that it taught.

If you were working as part of the battalion, then repeat the gist of the Commanding Officer's comments. This often cannot be done the same day, but it is a great deal better to do it two or three days afterwards than not to do it at all.

4. THE ENCOURAGEMENT OF INITIATIVE.

This is the corner-stone of successful training. In a Utopian Army every officer and non-commissioned officer would thirst for a chance to show initiative, and to act on his own responsibility. The predominance of our Navy (from a personnel point of view) among the navies of the world, is largely due to the existence of this spirit.

The tendency in armies is frequently the opposite—to shirk responsibility and to lean on stronger men. Who does not know the officer who secretly leans on his company sergeant-major, and when he has perforce to take a decision in the field between two rival courses invariably takes the line of least resistance.

It is true that this willingness to accept
responsibility is frequently, in many cases,
a gift, but it is equally true that it can be
acquired.   " Put a man on his own and he
will surprise himself " is no mere common-
place.

Consequently you as Officer Commanding
Company should be always " putting men on
their own " both as regards officers and non-
commissioned officers.   Whatever job you
give them to do *never interfere* whilst they
are doing it, unless the result will be harm-
ful to the men under them. Any interference
will curb their initiative.

Watch them at work, and at the " pow
wow " afterwards, criticise it (though not,
of course, in the presence of their men).

If the mistakes made are due to excess of
initiative, deal very gently with the errors.
If there is anything to praise in the work,
make the most of it; a little praise goes a
long way.

5. CONSIDER THE MEN'S COMFORT.

A poor battalion can generally be known
either by the way it leaves its lines after a
camp or bivouac, or by the hour it parades.

For example, a brigade is ordered to rendez-vous at a certain place at 10 a.m.   The battalion commander, who has 30 minutes march to get there, orders his battalion to parade at 9.   (He is fearful of anything going wrong.) The Officer Commanding Company orders his parade for 8.40 (likewise fearful of anything going wrong).   The section leader, equally anxious, turns his men out (" Just to see that all is right ") at 8.30.   The result is that for no object whatever the unfortunate soldier is kept on the go for 1½ hours where 50 minutes would have been ample.

Likewise, it is not essential to order a parade for the actual quarters of an hour.   A parade can be ordered for 6.25 just as well as 6.15, and ten minutes standing about for the men thereby avoided.

Much can be done for the men's comfort in the matter of avoiding unnecessary standing " to attention " and " marching to attention."   Insist on steadiness and smartness when standing " to attention " or marching " to attention "—slovenliness is the hall-mark of the bad soldier—but never keep the men at it unnecessarily.   Again, when giving instruction in the open, invariably let the men sit down.

Whenever the company is likely to be out much past the usual dinner hour, arrange for a '' haversack ration '' (bread and cheese) to be carried by each man.   Also, if late returning, send on a man ahead to warn the company cooks to have the dinners ready.

These things may appear details, but they will enable you to get much more out of the men when it is needed, and will strengthen the bond of sympathy between officers and men, which is a great aid to successful leadership.

WET WEATHER.

There is no advantage gained by carrying through the ordinary programme if the weather is bad.   Apart from the difficulty often experienced in getting clothes dried, especially in camp, the men will take but little interest in what is going on.   It is better to postpone the ordinary programme and to substitute another, viz., physical training, instruction in knots and lashings, lectures, bayonet fighting, miniature range practice, preparing a house for defence, duties in billets, and special instruction for officers and non-commissioned officers in writing reports and messages, map reading, etc.

CHAPTER V.

LEARNING TO ATTACK.

Skirmishing—Extended Order—Fire, Cover,
  and Use of Ground—Infantry in Attack—
  The Defence—Retirements.

Having discussed the general principles
which should underlie all training, we come
now to the actual details. We assume that
the company has been thoroughly instructed
in elementary drill and rifle exercises, and
probably has had some instruction in platoon drill; the men should also have had
instruction in " Care of Arms," " Parts of
the Rifle," " Aiming," " Firing Positions,"
and possibly a certain amount of " Elementary Theory of Musketry." They are now
ready to proceed to extended order, skirmishing and all that that leads to.

SKIRMISHING.

Every British infantry man is expected to
be a " good skirmisher." What does that
imply? It implies that he can move as one
of a section in extended order at the interval

required, either at a walk or run, and that whenever he is ordered to halt he will at once spot, and lie down behind any cover or fold in the ground close to him which will enable him to use his rifle effectively against the enemy, and yet expose to view as little of his body as possible.

We have already seen tributes of German officers and men to this feature of our infantry work; they could not believe troops could advance to the attack without showing themselves to any extent.

In training the recruit to this end, we must teach him first of all the Extended Order movements and the signals as a drill (I.T., Chapter V.).

EXTENDED ORDER.

He must learn what 2, 4, and 6 paces extension mean. When starting instruction in this, carry out the extensions from the centre; directly the extension " at the halt " is completed let the Section Commander step off the correct number of paces for each man from the centre man (another non-commissioned officer doing the same to the other flank)—do not let the men who have not hit off the right interval move, as that naturally puts the next man wrong—each man accordingly sees how far he is out, and should correct it next time.

Having got them to extend " at the halt " to two paces fairly correctly, signal the " Advance " and move them 200 yards or so, and then halt them and step off the intervals again ; when a fair result is shown proceed to four paces extension and later to six, carrying out the same system each time.

The object of this is to impress these intervals so strongly on the men's minds that when skirmishing they keep the approximately correct intervals unconsciously, and can devote all their time to taking advantage of the ground and to using their rifles to the best effect.

Practice should later be given in extending to a flank when marching in fours (I.T., Sec. 93, para. 2), and also in carrying out extensions by means of rough-and-ready expedients (I.T., Sec. 93, para. 1).

SIGNALS.

When practising the signals do not indulge in many "wheels" with the men in line ; the wheel is very easily learnt, and the manœuvre, if the line is a long one, is very hard work for the flank men.

Insist on all signals being given with the man who is signalling facing the front.

Having got the company fairly handy in this extended order work and in knowledge of the signals, you proceed to instruction in the other details that go to make up skirmishing—all this work is best done by sections, as larger units are cumbersome.

TAKING ADVANTAGE OF GROUND AND COVER.

Instruction in taking advantage of ground is best commenced by personal example, the section leader lying down in front of the section and taking up a good firing position either in a fold of the ground or behind cover.

It is a useful practice if in each section there are a few trained men who can skirmish. Let the section lie down, for preference on rising ground, and then let these men skirmish up to them (if the ground is '' broken '' better instruction is given); this gives the recruit a practical insight into the possibilities of skirmishing.

Nothing is needed now but practice to get the men handy; at every halt, when skirmishing, the section leader should at once open fire selecting distant objects up to about 1,000 yards, and frequently moving ones; this gives good practice to the non-commissioned officers in Fire Control and to the men in Fire Discipline.

LECTURES ON FIRE, COVER, AND USE OF GROUND.

This work should be accompanied by lectures on Fire (I.T., Secs. 116, 117, 118), and on Cover and the Use of Ground (I.T., Sec. 108).

A striking example of the effect of well-controlled and well-directed fire is to be seen in the terrific losses caused to the Germans through British infantry fire, notably at the battles of the Marne and the Aisne.

In lecturing on Cover emphasize the following points:—

1. The distinction between cover from "view" and cover from "fire."

2. The importance of the background and the avoidance of a possible ranging mark for the enemy's guns, viz., the edge of a wood or a hedge; the fact

that very often the best position for
a trench is right in the open, provided it is well concealed (i.e., made
to look like the surrounding ground).

3. The need for avoiding the " sky-line "
on all occasions.

4. Above all, the fact that the criterion
of good cover is not invisibility from
the enemy, but the effectiveness of the
fire you can bring to bear on the
enemy.

The Passing of Messages and Orders.

Thorough instructions as regards verbal
messages and orders are laid down in Infantry Training (1914), Sec. 96.

The importance of everyone being able to
pass a simple message or Fire Order correctly
can hardly be exaggerated. A single mistake on the part of one man may affect the
lives of many.

On active service the obvious need as regards the passing of messages is :—

1. To reduce messages to a minimum.

2. To pass them through as few people as
possible.

Nevertheless, there will be many occasions
when a written message is impossible and

where a verbal message has to be actually passed from man to man.

In lecturing the company on the subject on the lines of the above quoted section in Infantry Training, previous to practising it, emphasize strongly the direct prohibition that now exists as to sending a verbal order without saying whom it is from and whom it is intended for.

METHOD OF PRACTISING THE PASSING OF MESSAGES OR ORDERS.

The simplest way is to get each pair of sections arranged in a wide circle, with the non-commissioned officers and men at about 10 yards interval. Whisper a sample message to one man—*see that he understands it*—make him then repeat it to you.

When he can repeat it correctly, tell him to go and whisper it to his next-door neighbour on his left. Then start another message round the opposite way, beginning with the man on the right of the original man. Then go round with one of the messages, listening to each man's repetition of it, whilst the senior section commander goes round with the other; make careful note of where any mistake occurs; if in passing it gets so altered as to be senseless restart it correctly. Whilst the platoon commander, assisted by the senior section commander, are supervising one circle, the platoon sergeant, assisted by the senior section commander concerned, can supervise the other circle.

In the 8-company organization, whilst you are supervising one section, assisted by the section commander, each of your subalterns would be supervising one of their sections, and the colour-sergeant would undertake the fourth section.

When both messages have gone round you then draw attention to the faults and carelessness displayed, warn the offenders to be more careful, and then repeat the practice with two more messages.

After this you will have a clear idea of the weak men, and should arrange for extra practice for them out of parade hours.

There are two points of special importance in this practice—

1. Let the message be practical—a simple one that might really be sent.

2. Insist on every man understanding the message before passing it on.

PASSING OF FIRE ORDER.

Where it is possible on service, fire orders will either be shouted or passed from section commander to section commander, or non-commissioned officer to non-commissioned officer. But often when the noise is great it will be necessary to pass them down from man to man. This can be practised in the same way as messages. Rapidity is of great importance and a good deal of "speeding up" will be necessary when accuracy is reached.

FURTHER PRACTICE.

Practice in passing both messages and orders should now be continued on all skirmishing practices, when practising the Attack, in Field Firing Practices, and whenever blank ammunition is used.

INFANTRY IN ATTACK.

The preliminary work now being accomplished, you would start the company on the Attack (I.T., Secs. 121—124).

For purposes of instruction it will be found best to divide an ordinary attack roughly into three periods—

1. The advance up to the first fire position.
2. The Fire Fight, or struggle for superiority of fire.

3. The Assault and Pursuit.

1. ADVANCE TO THE FIRST FIRE POSITION.

You would explain that where possible the attackers would move under cover; if that was not possible, they would adopt a formation which has been found to be less vulnerable to shrapnel fire than any other, i.e., small shallow columns (viz., platoons in column of fours) on an irregular front, with not less than 50 yards interval,* and 200 yards distance between each line, and scouts out in front. The point of this formation is that at long ranges, over 1,400 yards or so, you cannot damage the enemy with rifle fire to any extent, nor he you; consequently the sole object is to suffer as little as possible from his guns. This formation would have to give place to lines of skirmishers directly the enemy's rifle or machine gun fire began to take effect; the scouts then lie down and wait till the firing line comes up and absorbs them.

2. THE FIRE FIGHT.

The chief points you would draw attention to under this heading are:—

_____

*Interval is the lateral space between men or units, distance is the vertical space from front to rear.

(1.) The need for effective artillery support to enable the infantry to make ground, the artillery " searching " the enemy's trenches with shrapnel and keeping the defenders' heads down.

(2.) The need for covering fire, (*a*) of one company or platoon covering with its fire the advance of its neighbours, (*b*) of special detachments of infantry posted, if possible, on a flank (see I.T., 1914, Sec. 121, para. 8).

(3.) The need for a steady, accurate hail of lead on the enemy's trenches.

(4.) The need for every officer, non-commissioned officer, and man to be imbued with one desire, namely, to get to close quarters with the enemy as quickly as possible.

(5.) The need for constant reinforcing (as a rule a platoon at a time) as required from the lines in rear, namely, first the Supports, and, when they are used up, the Local Reserves. Thus is the Firing Line thickened up until it reaches its maximum density the last few hundred yards of the attack, when development of the greatest possible volume of fire outweighs every other

consideration. Each man of the rein-
forcements, as he reaches the Firing
Line, should at once be told by his
neighbours the target and the range.

(6.) The need for the utmost attention
being paid to keeping the direction—in
each company a non-commissioned
officer should be specially detailed for
this alone.

(7.) The need for short rushes (anything
from 10 to 30 yards) by platoons, sections, or groups of men
as the attackers get to close range
—roughly the last 600 yards. These
rushes have to be most carefully
practised in order to ensure their
being made altogether; a very small
target is thus presented to the enemy,
which is not the case if the men do
not rise or drop together. It is a good
system for the non-commissioned officer
to shout out (and for the men to pass
down) the words " Prepare to rush "
immediately before a rush. On that
every man ceases fire and puts over his
safety catch, and looks to the non-
commissioned officer, who then shouts
" Rush," and leads the section to the

next point, which he has already
spotted whilst lying down.

(8.) The need for all section commanders
to form impromptu sections as rein-
forcements arrive. Many men of other
sections, and often other companies,
come up and get mixed with the men
of the original section. The sergeant
should instruct the men on his right
and left, roughly 12 to 15 all told
(regardless of their section or company) to come forward with him at the
next advance. He should also warn
any non-commissioned officers he sees
on his right and left to do likewise,
carrying on from his flank men.
Should the attackers reach some dead
ground during the advance, and
should time allow, companies should
seize the opportunity of re-forming.

3. THE ASSAULT AND PURSUIT.

There is nothing to add under this heading
to Sec. 124, Infantry Training.

The above will give an idea of how best
to instruct the Company in the all-important

subject of the Attack. It has been treated
in this somewhat dogmatic way to make the
subject easy of comprehension, but it should
be pointed out that there is no such thing as
a stereotyped form of attack, and that as
long as the main principle is acted on, i.e.,
a resolute advance, and a gradual beating
down of the enemy's opposition by steady,
accurate fire, supported by artillery, machine
guns, and possibly detachments on a flank,
with the object of getting so close to the position that a bayonet charge can be delivered,
it matters but little exactly what form the
attack takes.

In practising the Attack, three parts of the
time available should be devoted to the Fire-
fight period, and the time given to this should
under no circumstances be scamped.

In any such scheme where both sides are
represented, it will add very greatly to the
success of it, if both sides are issued with
blank ammunition, the "skeleton" force
having, say, 15 rounds per man, and the
remainder of the company five rounds.

After the attack has been fairly satisfac-
torily carried out without an enemy, arrange
for one platoon (or section) to act as a
"skeleton" enemy, and to take up a position

for the other three platoons to attack. When practising the Attack with another company, carry the practice right through to its logical conclusion, including the assault, the re-forming, and the pursuit.

OTHER ARMS OF THE SERVICE.

Before proceeding further with the Field Training it will be as well to give one or two lectures to the company on the rôle in war and the organisation of the other arms of the Service (F.S.R., Part I., Chap. 1).

DEFENCE.

(I.T., Secs. 125-133.)

Although the defence of a position involves questions of the greatest importance to officers and to a less extent non-commissioned officers, viz., the selection of the position, the strength of the flanks, the possibilities of counter-attack, and the steps to be taken to improve the position, little time need be spent under present circumstances by the Company as a whole in practising the defence.

The practical work of taking up a position of defence should be postponed until instruction has been given in Entrenching (see page 92).

At the same time it will be as well to draw attention to the great principle underlying all Active Defence, namely the Offensive Defensive—in other words the Counter-Attack (excellent examples of which were displayed by the Germans in the Battle of the Aisne, September—October, 1914)—and further to explain the rôle of the Supports, Local Reserve, and General Reserve in defence.

RETIREMENTS.

(See I.T., Sec. 137.)

This subject requires a great deal of practice, as it is admittedly the most difficult operation to carry out in war. It needs almost a genius to know when to retire; hang on too long and you are likely to be cut off—retire too quickly and the retirement is likely to turn into a rout. There is no branch of military activity in which the *moral* and training of troops is so severely tested—hence the need for much practice.

What will, no doubt, in the history of the future, be looked upon as a classic retirement was that of the British Expeditionary Force from Mons to the outskirts of Paris (August 26th-29th), when outnumbered by three to one and entirely unsupported. There was every reason for the capture, or, at any rate, the utter rout, of a large part of this force, but good leadership, excellent training and *moral* on the part of the officers, non-commissioned officers and men, succeeded in averting any disaster.

From a company point of view, however, the time devoted to " Retirements " need not be long.

The essential points to see to are as follow : —

1. Impress the fact on all ranks that a successful retirement is largely a question of " *moral* "—in other words of " keeping your head." There is always a danger in retirement of certain men losing their heads and thinking only of escape; such an example is liable to spread with disastrous consequences.

2. Retirements should be slow and steady. If, however, open ground has to be crossed within close range of the enemy, it should naturally be crossed as rapidly as possible.

3. Much depends on good fire positions being selected in retirement; a good field of fire is essential.

4. Retirements should be made piecemeal —for instance, say a company is carrying out a retirement; let half the company go back first, and establish itself on the next fire position; directly that is done let the other half company retire, leaving, however, eight or ten men, who are good runners, behind. These men keep up a rapid and sustained fire, the better to deceive the enemy.

The half company who are now on their way back, and later the final party, must take care to avoid "masking" the fire of the other half-company who are occupying the new position.

5. Mutual support by the fire of one platoon or half-company covering the movement of another should be employed as much in retirement as in attack.

A lecture should be given, explaining how the retirement of a mixed force of all arms would be carried out, i.e., the distinctive rôle of the Cavalry, Artillery, Engineers, and Machine Guns (F.S.R., Part I., Secs. 71-72). An excellent illustration of artillery work in a retirement is furnished by the action of the British Artillery in the retreat from Mons

(August 26th-29th), where they were opposed to the artillery of five army corps, and yet were so well handled, that, at very heavy cost, they enabled General Smith-Dorrien's Army Corps to extricate itself when almost overwhelmed.

CHAPTER VI.

PROTECTION.

General Principles—Rôle of Different Arms—
 Infantry Advanced Guard—Infantry Rear
 Guard and Flank Guard.

It has frequently been found by instructors that the subject of Protection is a fruitful source of worry to the military beginner. The only reason to account for this is the large number of terms involved, such as Piquets, Sentry Groups, Supports, Van Guards, etc., all of which are potential stumbling-blocks to the recruit.

Consequently it is advisable before starting this subject to impress this fact—that Protection, like tactics, is *based entirely on common-sense*.

For some reason or other many people without military experience find it hard to believe that anything to do with the Art of War can be merely common-sense, and it is no easy matter to convince them. The method of instruction on this subject varies a good deal, but the following method is recommended.

METHOD OF INSTRUCTION.

1. Start with a lecture on the General Principles of Protection, showing also roughly the rôle of the different arms in Protection on the march, and in Protection when at rest. This will afford the company a general idea of all Protection.

2. Continue the subject with a lecture on an Infantry Advanced Guard.

3. Practise the same, using a man with a flag to denote the Main Body.

4. Treat an Infantry Rear Guard and Flank Guard the same way, first of all giving a lecture on the subject, and then practising it in the field.

5. Proceed now to Protection when at rest—in other words, Outposts. Possibly two lectures will be required to make intelligible the divisions of an Outpost force and the duties of the different parts.

6. Practise elementary Outposts, dividing the whole company up into sentry groups, thus ensuring that everyone shall know what is expected of him when acting as an Outpost sentry.

7. Practise the work of a sample Outpost Company. This will need to be done on

E 2

several occasions and must on no account be hurried.

We will now offer a few suggestions on the above headings :—

1. LECTURE ON GENERAL PRINCI- PLES OF PROTECTION.

Points to be made :—

(1) Endeavour to look upon Protection on the march and outposts as identical in principle ; the various Guards (Advanced, Rear, and Flank) have been sometimes termed "moving outposts."

(2) The need for every force from an Army Corps to an Infantry Section, whether moving or at rest, being adequately protected by a smaller force. (Instances can be given from the early part of the South African War where the outposts were not adequate, and the result was disaster.)

(3) The reason why troops on the move or at rest cannot defend themselves— on the march troops adopt the only convenient formation for moving along roads, viz. Infantry, column

of fours; Cavalry, column of sections or half-sections; Artillery, column of route.

These formations are obviously the worst possible for defence. Therefore some force must be sent out to prevent the enemy attacking the column whilst in their march formations—this force is known as Advanced, Rear, or Flank Guards, according to the direction in which it is sent out.

Likewise in the matter of Outposts, troops when at rest must be given the most complete rest possible, and it is obviously more convenient from every point of view to have them concentrated in a small area. Consequently a force must be detailed to protect them from the enemy, prevent their being disturbed, and, in the case of serious attack, afford time for them to get from the rest formation to a fighting one; in other words, deploy.

(4) The necessity of restricting protective troops to the fewest number possible on account of the exhausting nature of protective work. The usual proportion is from one-eighth to one-fourth of the force.

(5) The vital necessity for all protective forces in the event of attack, at any risk to themselves, gaining sufficient time for the Main Body to prepare to meet the attack.

(6) The need for giving the Commander of the protective force a *free hand* as to his dispositions, viz. : if you, as Officer Commanding Main Body, instruct an Advanced Guard Commander what distance ahead he is to keep, and a disaster ensues, you become largely, if not wholly, responsible for it.

(7) The responsibility of the commander of the protective force for maintaining connection with his Main Body.

(8) The need for local infantry protection whatever cavalry "screen" may happen to be in front.

THE RÔLE OF THE DIFFERENT ARMS IN PROTECTION.

Cavalry—

(1) General protective duties some distance ahead of each column, providing a kind of screen.

(2) Special missions—mostly of a reconnaissance nature.

(3) Divisional duties, i.e., they act as the leading troops in an Advanced Guard and as the rearmost troops in a Rear Guard (with the special duty of guarding the flanks), and they carry out the reconnaissance work of outposts by day.

Artillery—

(1) Provide the main striking power in the various guards, thereby keeping the enemy at a respectful distance.

(2) Only occasionally used with Outposts, viz., if there is limited ground over which the enemy must pass, if it is important to prevent the enemy seizing artillery positions within close range of the Main Body, or if the Outposts occupy the ground which the Main Body is to hold in case of attack.

Engineers.—Always employed with Advanced Guard, to repair any bridges or portions of the road needing it, clear away obstacles, etc.; also with the Rear Guard, making obstacles to hinder the enemy's advance, laying ambushes, and on certain occasions blowing up bridges and destroying boats, etc.

Infantry.—Responsible for the main resistance both on protection on the march and on outpost duty.

2. INFANTRY ADVANCED GUARD.

It should now be clear to everyone that normally an Advanced Guard is composed of all arms, but there will be occasions, as for instance the march of an Infantry Brigade or Battalion, when there will not be any other arms to assist in the protection of the Main Body.

The best method of instruction in " telling off " an Infantry Advanced, Rear, or Flank Guard is by drawing a simple diagram showing the distribution and relative position of the different portions of the guard (see Diagram I.).   No amount of explanation will answer the same purpose.

If you have no blackboard and no paper, chalk it on a table or scratch it on the ground ; it is a matter of no concern how rough or untidy it is, as long as it is clear. Having by this means impressed on the

DIAGRAM I.

INFANTRY ADVANCED GUARD
(½-Company)

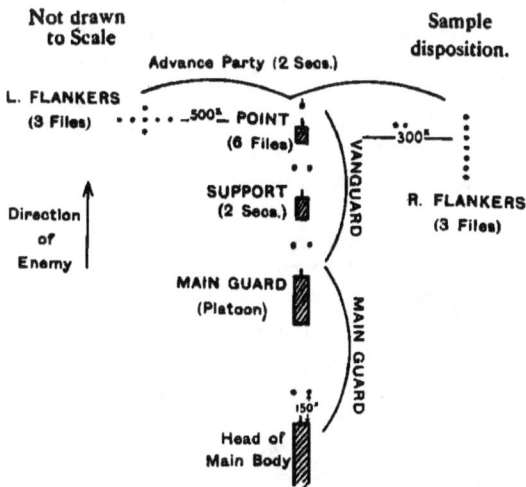

Not drawn to Scale

Sample disposition.

Advance Party (2 Secs.)

L. FLANKERS (3 Files) · · · · · __500ˣ__ POINT (6 Files)

__300ˣ__

VANGUARD

R. FLANKERS (3 Files)

Direction of Enemy

SUPPORT (2 Secs.)

MAIN GUARD (Platoon)

MAIN GUARD

150ˣ

Head of Main Body

NOTES.

(a) · · denote one connecting file.
(b) Country on right flank of advance is wooded; hence the formation and distance away of R. flankers.
(c) Country on left flank of advance is open; hence the formation and distance away of L. Flankers.
(d) The numbers shewn above under the different headings are given merely as a possible distribution, and are not intended as in any way binding.

company what an Advanced Guard looks like when put out, it is advisable then to take the case of a Battalion about to move '' on its own,'' with one company detailed for Advanced Guard.

The Company Commander will first make a point of finding out, if he has not already been told—

(1) What is known of the enemy and other parts of his own force.

(2) What the intentions of his Battalion Commander are, the route, etc.

(3) What amount of resistance he is to make if he meets the enemy.

(4) What time the Main Body leaves the '' starting point.''

Having satisfied himself on these points, he will make up his mind how he will distribute the company, and what time each portion must move off; that will, of course, depend on the distance ahead they are to keep. How is he to settle that? The distance depends considerably on the nature of the country; if open, they will need to be far ahead; if close with no lengthy view possible, they would be a shorter distance. He must at all hazards prevent the enemy firing on the Main Body at effective range, i.e., anything less than 1,400 yards; if there is any danger of meeting Artillery this distance should be nearly doubled. It is therefore impossible to lay down any rule, but we may take 1,000 yards as quite a normal distance for the head of the Main Guard to be ahead of the Main Body in an Infantry force; the support of the Van Guard might be 300 yards further ahead and the Advance Party 200 yards still further.

He must, therefore, so despatch the different portions of his Advanced Guard that they will be strung out in their proper position by the time that the Main Body leaves the starting point.

As to distribution, the most convenient system is to detail one half-company as Van Guard, furnishing Advance Party and Support and the necessary connecting files (who should not be more than 200 yards apart), and the other half company as Main Guard, who will be responsible for keeping up connection with the Main Body; if the Officer Commanding Main Guard finds he is getting out of touch at any time with the Main Body all he has to do is to drop more connecting files.

Note.—Connection must be maintained from front to rear, i.e., Officer Commanding Van Guard is responsible for his connection with the Main Guard, and Officer Commanding Main Guard for his connection with the Main Body; at the same time this does not relieve the Officer Commanding Main Body of responsibility for taking necessary steps to see that communication is maintained.

The Officers commanding the respective half-companies on being told off to their rôles, immediately tell off their commands accordingly, viz., the Officer Commanding Van Guard would normally tell off one platoon as Advance Party and one platoon as Support; the Officer in charge of the Advance Party would at once tell off a party for Point, and other parties for Right and Left Flankers respectively, leaving only a connecting file to connect with the Support. (See Diagram I.)

As to the formation of these small parties, it is best for the Point to open out and march each side of the road, with one of their number as scout about two hundred yards to the front.

The Flankers would move level to the Point a few hundred yards away on either flank, the distance being entirely a question of the nature of the country and the view obtainable. If in open country, an open diamond formation is a good one; if moving through woods or cover of any sort, single file will probably be best.

It should be impressed on the company that the chief duty of the van guard is reconnaissance, and that of the main guard resistance.

ADVANCED GUARD TO A FORCE RETIRING.

So far we have assumed that the force is advancing. In the case of a force retiring it is also necessary to detail an Advanced Guard. Their duty is obviously far less important, and a very small body can carry it out; still it must not be ignored. A good instance of ignoring it was seen in the South African War at the battle of Sanna's Post, where disaster overtook the British force through the neglect of this precaution.

3. PRACTISING AN INFANTRY ADVANCED GUARD.

Having thoroughly explained the Infantry Advanced Guard by lecture and diagram, it only remains to carry it out practically. For this purpose it is essential that the Officer Commanding company should be mounted, either on horseback or bicycle. It is a good practice to instruct the Officer Commanding Van Guard to send back from the Advance Party frequent signals (viz. " No enemy in sight ") and to make a note of each one sent and the time; the man with the flag (preferably a non-commissioned officer) representing the main body, to make a note of the arrival of the signal and the time.

It is also a good practice to pass down simple verbal messages under the same system; thus the company can be tested in passing signals and messages accurately and rapidly.

It will be found advisable to warn everyone against starting signals on their own account; otherwise when a connecting file sees a party halted in front he might signal "the halt" back, and so delay the whole Advanced Guard; secondly, warn everyone that the man who passes the signal must *satisfy himself* that the man to whom he sends it understands the signals sent; this he knows by watching the latter pass it on correctly.

As regards the question of " pace," the great object is to enable the Main Body to move at the ordinary marching pace, 3 miles per hour. It will occasionally happen that the Flankers are handicapped by having to traverse rough country; this must not, however, be allowed to delay the whole guard, and it will occasionally be advisable, if the flankers are dropping back, to send out fresh ones, the old ones being told to rejoin the column.

In practising the various guards, an endeavour should be made to give each section experience, at one time or another, of the different divisions of the guard.

4. LECTURE.—INFANTRY REAR GUARD AND FLANK GUARD.

Demonstrate by diagram (Diagrams II., III., IV.).

It will save much confusion if the fact is impressed on the Company that the Rear Guard is practically the same as an Advanced Guard the other way round, the only differences of importance being that the Rear Guard as a rule has no Support, being divided merely into Rear Party and Main Guard), and that at any halt every memb r of the

DIAGRAM II.

INFANTRY REAR GUARD,
To a Force Retiring *
(½-Company)

Not drawn
to Scale

Sample
Disposition

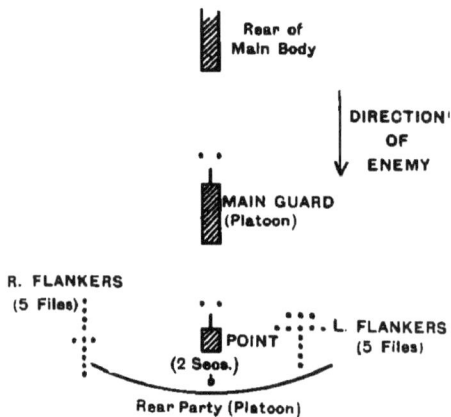

Rear of
Main Body

DIRECTION
OF
ENEMY

MAIN GUARD
(Platoon)

R. FLANKERS
(5 Files)

POINT

L. FLANKERS
(5 Files)

(2 Secs.)

Rear Party (Platoon)

NOTES.

(a) ˙ ˙ denote one connecting file.

(b) The number of connecting files depends entirely on the distance that the various bodies are apart; each file should not have to cover more than 150 to 200 yards.

(c) The formation in which the flankers move and their distance from the Point depends firstly on the nature of the country, secondly on the proximity and position of the enemy.

*(d) If the force were advancing, the only difference as a rule would be the size of the Rear Guard, which would probably be half as strong.

(e) The numbers shown above under the different headings are given merely as a possible distribution, and are not intended as in any way binding.

DIAGRAM III.

INFANTRY FLANK GUARD.
(½-Company)

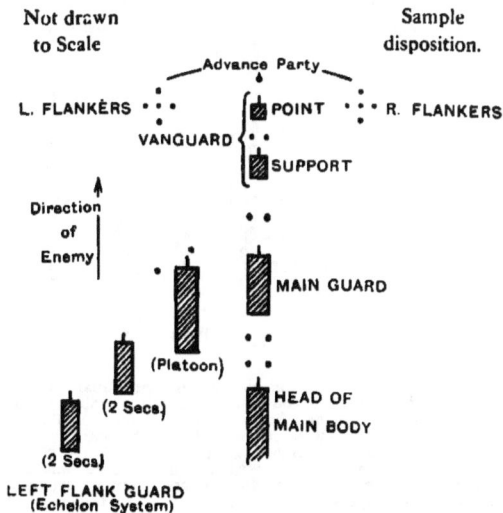

Not drawn
to Scale

Sample
disposition.

Advance Party

L. FLANKERS • • • ☑ POINT • • • R. FLANKERS

VANGUARD { • • •
☑ SUPPORT

Direction
of
Enemy

• •
☐ MAIN GUARD

• •

• •

☐ (Platoon)

☐ (2 Secs)

☐ HEAD OF
MAIN BODY

(2 Secs)

LEFT FLANK GUARD
(Echelon System)

R. T.   F

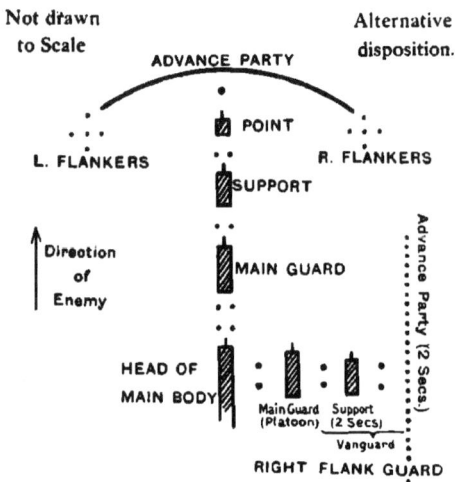

DIAGRAM IV.

INFANTRY FLANK GUARD
(½-Company)

(a) Two methods of putting out moving Flank Guards are here shown. The actual position would be purely a matter for O.C. Flank Guard to decide; he is responsible for guarding the threatened flank; he is unfettered as to how he does it.

(b) . . denote one connecting file.

(c) In the echelon flank guard shown above, it might be necessary to have connecting files; in open country they could probably be dispensed with; in close country they would be needed.

(d) The numbers shown above under the different headings are given merely as a possible distribution, and are not intended as in any way binding.

Rear Guard should turn about and face his real front, i.e., the enemy.

It should also be pointed out that a Rear Guard should always be detailed, no matter whether the force is retiring or advancing; in the latter case it would not need to be nearly as strong as the Advanced Guard; in the former it would as a rule be about a quarter of the whole force.

FLANK GUARD.

In speaking about a Flank Guard, it should be emphasized that whereas Advanced and Rear Guards are at all times essential, a Flank Guard is not so. It is only detailed if there is a danger of an attack from one or other flank.

If there are no parallel roads to the route of the column, it is customary to send out a stationary Flank Guard either to some important cross-roads or road junction on the flank of the main route, or possibly to some commanding ground which must be denied to the enemy ; in this case directly the column has passed, the Flank Guard would join the rear of the column.

If, however, there is a convenient parallel road, and the situation calls for a Flank

Guard, a special force would be detailed for that purpose.   The Commander would be given an absolutely free hand as to his dispositions.

In the case of an Infantry force " on its own," the commander of the Flank Guard would similarly decide his own formation. The most common one is " echelon," which is hard to explain, but easy to depict (see Diagram III.).

This is very suitable in open ground, but not so suitable if the country is close; in that case it would often be best to have a platoon in single file well out (possibly 800 to 1,000 yards) on the flank, with scouts still further out to the flank, another platoon in column of fours in support, and the other half-company in column of fours half-way between them and the Main Body; connecting files, of course, would be required.

PRACTISING INFANTRY REAR GUARD AND FLANK GUARD.

It is advisable to have a man with a flag representing the Main Body.   After both Rear Guard and Flank Guard have been practised without an enemy, tell off one section to act as a "skeleton" enemy, and to make a surprise attack on the company on its march; arrange for blank ammunition if possible. This is excellent practice for testing the initiative of your subalterns and section commanders. On such occasions as these, Officers and non-commissioned officers should be trained to act promptly; the obvious object is to get the men extended at lightning speed, and to open fire as rapidly as possible; hence any kind of drill is utterly out of place. Some such order as the following —"Line that bank—scatter." Then "Quarter Right—At the enemy in the bushes—500—rapid—fire" is all that is needed.

Frequent practice will be required in dealing with these impromptu situations, especially for the Officers and non-commissioned officers. It is advisable in the case of Flank Guards to practise all three different kinds mentioned in the lecture above.

CHAPTER VII.

THE COMPANY ON OUTPOST.

(I.T., 1914, Chapter XIV.)

Lecture on Outposts—Practising Elementary Outposts—Outpost Company Scheme—Duties of Outpost Company Commander and of Piquet Commander.

LECTURE ON OUTPOSTS.

(Illustrated by rough Diagram (see Diagram V.)).

Points to be made:—

1. The definite allotment of a certain piece of ground to each Outpost Company for the defence of which the Company would be entirely responsible.

2. The fact that in selecting the position of the piquets resistance is of greater importance than a commanding view. A good field of fire for, if possible, 300 yards is of vital importance.

3. The entire option of the Company

Commander in deciding how to distribute his company, viz., whether he has 2 piquets, 1 support, and a detached post, or 1 piquet, 1 support, without a detached post, or any other arrangement. It is entirely a question of ground, the possibilities for defence, and the facilities for getting quickly from one portion of it to another; the main principle being not to divide up the company more than necessary.

4. The fact that the piquet line is as a general rule the line of resistance, on account of the danger, especially at night, of retirements of advanced troops on to a supporting line. In case of attack, therefore, the supports reinforce the piquets, instead of the latter falling back on the supports.

5. The fact that special arrangements have to be made for night; the roads, tracks, and footpaths leading to the front become then of primary importance, and must be carefully guarded. In most cases the piquets and sentry groups would be moved from their day position on to the roads, paths, etc.. by which the enemy might attack.

DIAGRAM V.

OUTPOST POSITION BY DAY *
(1 Outpost Company)

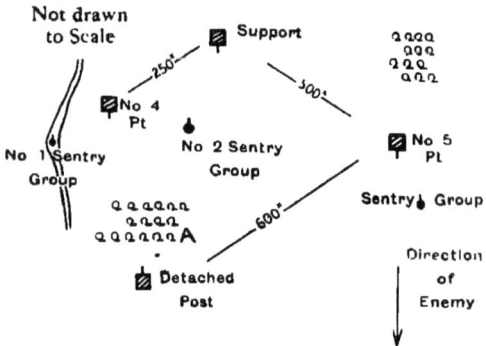

Not drawn
to Scale

Support

No 4
Pt

250"

500"

No 1 Sentry
Group

No 2 Sentry
Group

No 5
Pl

Sentry Group

600"

A

Detached
Post

Direction
of
Enemy

NOTES TO DIAGRAM V.

(*a*) A sample Outpost company in the middle of the line of Outposts ; its limits are from the road (inclusive) on the right, to the wood on the left flank of the position (exclusive).

It furnishes two piquets, one detached post, and one support. No. 4 Pt. is finding two sentry groups, No. 5. is finding one sentry group.

(Piquets are usually numbered from the right of the line of outposts.)

(*b*) The detached post is required because of the opportunity that would otherwise be afforded the enemy of collecting in wood marked A.

No. 5 Piquet's trench will be so sited as to bring an effective oblique fire to bear on the ground the far side of wood A. This covering fire will materially help the detached post, and, in the event of their being forced back, will cover their retirement. If wood A were further from the line of piquets it would be a mistake to place a detached post there on account of the danger of it being cut off.

(c) By night the Piquets and Sentry-Groups would be moved to the roads, tracks, footpaths, etc. leading to the front. A standing patrol of mounted men, cyclists, or infantry, would very likely be stationed at any road junction, or cross-roads, on the road shewn on the right flank of the position at a distance of anything up to a mile from the piquet line.

6. The need for telling off a detached post in the case of an outpost company on the flank, where there is danger of having the flank turned, or in front of the sentry line to watch some spot where the enemy might collect unseen. It should be pointed out that a detached post should not be told off unless absolutely necessary, on account of the danger of its being cut off.

7. The need for telling off Outpost patrols hitherto known as " Reconnoitring " patrols (two reliefs) for patrolling the country to the front of the position by night. By day this duty would be carried out by the Cavalry allotted to the Outposts or by cyclists, unless the country is very thick, or the weather misty, in which cases the Infantry would furnish the patrols.

8. The system of standing patrols, consisting of two to eight mounted men, cyclists, or Infantry sent out well in advance of the Outpost position to watch either the principal approaches or some particular points where the enemy could collect unseen.

9. The necessity for the piquet or detached post at once entrenching itself on

arriving at its position.   Supports
would also normally entrench unless
they had natural cover.

10. *The sentry-group system and the
duties of the sentry.

Note.—It may be as well for the benefit
of the old soldier to point out that both
Visiting Patrols and Examining Posts are
things of the past, the duties of the latter
being now performed by the piquets.

ELEMENTARY OUTPOSTS
PRACTISED.

The company should now have a fair
knowledge of the subject as far as explanation and diagram can give it.

The next step is to practise it — first by
giving the whole company experience of
sentry work, and secondly by carrying out
a complete Outpost Company scheme.

For purposes of convenience and instruction it may be best to have, independent of
one another, two sentry lines, if on rising
ground one above the other ; if on flat ground
one line facing one way and one the other.

---

* Infantry Training, 1914, makes no reference to the alterna-
tive method of posting sentries, i.e., direct from the piquet.
Consequently this method may be regarded as done away with.

The position of the piquets should be marked by single men or by flags. Each group should have a definite front to watch, and the non-commissioned officer or old soldier in charge of the group, should be held responsible for the sentry's knowledge of those matters which it is his business to know (viz., the position of the sentries on his right and left, position of the piquet and support, etc., etc.—I.T., Secs. 151, 152).

In order to give every man a turn on sentry, it is as well to change the sentries frequently, say every 10 or 15 minutes.

It is desirable to impress on the sentries—

(1) That they are absolutely responsible for the safety of the entire force as far as watching their particular portion of front is concerned, and that any movement of any description should be at once reported to the non-commissioned officer or old soldier in charge of the group.

(2) That the job of sentries is observation, not resistance; a sentry should only fire his rifle in the last resource.

(3) That it is essential to keep hidden as far as possible, consistent with observation, and to avoid moving.

The company having now been thoroughly instructed in actual sentry work, it only remains to carry out a few Outpost Company schemes.

OUTPOST COMPANY SCHEME.

For this purpose it is best to carry out the scheme exactly as it would be done on Active Service.

You assume that your company has been detached to take its place in an Outpost line; whether you are part of a Section of Outposts (as in the case of a large force) or not, makes no difference to the Outpost Company dispositions.

You have received orders, either verbally, or in writing, as to the limits of the ground allotted to you, also instructions on the various points of importance detailed in I.T., Chap. XIV. You march your company towards the ground allotted, preceded by a screen of scouts about half a mile ahead. You halt the company under cover, if possible, slightly in rear of the line to be taken up.

You then, accompanied by a subaltern and a non-commissioned officer, preferably the Company Sergeant-Major, walk over the

ground allotted to you.   (If pressed for time
it would be best to ride.)   You make up your
mind how best to occupy the position, i.e.,
the number of piquets, etc.

We assume that you consider two piquets,
one support and a detached post advisable,
and you decide exactly where to place them.
You then decide how you will distribute
your company; in this case it would be convenient to detail a platoon for each piquet
and the support, and the remaining one to
furnish the detached post and the two outpost patrols that will be required.   Always
endeavour to split up your platoons as little
as possible.

You then return to the company and tell
off the platoons to their various duties.
Before the company separate you should instruct them as to:—

1. What to do in case of attack (viz.,
   hold the piquet line till reinforced).

2. What friendly cavalry there are to the
   front.

3. The probable direction of the enemy.

4. Any special arrangements for the night
   (viz., moving a piquet on to a road).

5. Special rules as to smoking, lighting
   fires, or cooking, viz., often fires

would be allowed in the support line
but not in the piquet line.

6. The hour at which the Outposts will be
relieved.

7. Your own position.

You would further confidentially tell the
platoon commanders what the " private signal " or countersign is, and you would
warn all ranks to get a clear mental picture
of their surroundings while daylight lasts.

You then despatch the various platoons to
their respective tasks; the Officer and non-
commissioned officer who accompanied you
when looking over the ground might each
lead a piquet to its position, whilst you
decide on the position for the support.

That done, you might accompany the
detached post to their position and ensure
their being well placed, after which you
would visit the sentries and see that the
whole front was watched and that there was
no interval unwatched between your piquets
and those of the companies on either side of
you.

PIQUET COMMANDER'S TASK.

On arrival at the spot decided on by you,
the piquet commander would immediately

select the actual line for his trench, mark it out, and start his platoon digging. Directly he has done that, he would go over the ground allotted to him and decide on the number of sentry posts required and their position.

He would then return to his piquet, detail a sentry over the piquet, with two reliefs, and detail his sentry groups, consisting as a rule of one non-commissioned officer, or old soldier, and three men each.

He would then post his sentry groups.

A word as to the position of the sentry groups with the relation to the piquet. The sole object of the sentry is " watching." Therefore he must be placed where he can see well.

It may so happen that it will be necessary to post the groups 300-400 yards ahead of the piquet, but that would be the extreme limit, and very rarely would such a case occur. On the other hand, the sentry might get the best view 50 yards ahead of the piquet or even in line with it, and in some cases (viz., a piquet placed on a steep slope), he might be actually behind the piquet ; or again, the sentry might be placed up a tree with the remainder of the group at the base

of it. It is purely a matter of making the
best use of the ground.

Again as to the number of sentry
groups. This is entirely a question of
the view obtainable, and the amount of
front that the sentry can watch. If the
ground is absolutely open, one sentry group
may be all that is required; on the other
hand, in close country as many as three
might be required for each piquet. More
sentries will be required by night than by
day.

Needless to say, no more men should be
used on sentry work than absolutely necessary.

Before leaving a group he would satisfy
himself that the non-commissioned officer or
man in charge thoroughly knew his duties,
including the " private signal " or countersign. He would also definitely allot the
amount of front for which each sentry group
was responsible—for this purpose he must
co-operate with the piquets on either side
of him. He would further make sure that
the group was well hidden from the front.

He would then return to the piquet.

Recall Screen of Scouts.

Directly the entrenchments are completed

you will call in the screen of scouts which has been protecting your company from attack during the occupation of the position.

COMMUNICATION.

You should be careful to see that there is good communication between the supports and the piquet, and make sure that there is little danger of the supports losing themselves if summoned to reinforce the piquet line by night.

OUTPOST PATROLS.

In day time it would not, as a rule, be necessary to send out any outpost patrols, provided you knew the cavalry were patrolling only a short distance ahead, unless the country was very thick or the weather misty ; by night it would always be necessary.

HOSTILE PATROLS.

On every occasion that outposts are practised by day or night, arrangements should be made for hostile patrols to '' worry the outposts.''

CHAPTER VIII

FIELD ENGINEERING.

Essential Subjects—(a) for Whole Company, (b) for Officers and Sergeants—Special Training for Officers and Sergeants—Lecture—Progressive Digging—Issuing Tools—Extension of Working Party—Entrenching Implement—Competition—Various Forms of Trench—Drainage and Latrines—Protection Against Artillery Fire—Head Cover—Overhead Cover—Dummy Parapets—Obstacles—Clearance of Foreground—Knots and Lashings.

It is improbable in the circumstances of the case that very much time can be devoted to this subject. It is therefore especially important to decide what are the really important matters which are essential for the company to be instructed in before they are fit to take the field.

They may be summarised as follows:—

Every non-commissioned officer and man should be able:—

1. To extend as one of a working party carrying a pick and shovel, by day or night without confusion or noise.

G 2

To dig for four hours by day or night in average soil, and excavate 80 cubic feet of earth in the time without excessive fatigue.

3. To make the utmost use of the entrenching implement which he carries on him.

4. When lying down, to excavate rapidly sufficient soil to give him bullet-proof protection in that position.

5. To do his share in constructing head-cover, loopholes, and overhead cover, and in concealing a trench.

6. To take his part in erecting wire entanglements.

7. To tie a few simple knots and lashings; this can be taught on wet days, when work in the field is impracticable.

If, in addition to these qualifications, there is time to teach him how to "revet" the interior slope of a trench, and also a few bridging expedients, so much the better. Practical experience should also be given him in the clearance of foreground and in providing range marks.

An officer should be qualified to supervise all the above, and in addition should be able—

1. To site trenches to the best advantage.

   On no subject has military science received such a shock during the present war as on the subject of siting of trenches.

   We are now told on high authority that it is "madness" to site trenches on the forward slope of a hill; your trenches are quickly discovered, and you are literally shelled out in no time.

   Consequently you have perforce to site your trenches on the reverse slope. This will probably mean a sacrifice of a good field of fire, but it is held that even if you are restricted to a field of fire of 100 yards, it is better to place your trenches on the reverse slope rather than on the forward one.

2. To trace the outlines of a trench, allot the men's tasks, and start a party working by day or night with rapidity and without noise.

3. To supervise the construction of a simple fire trench, an improved fire trench, a "traversed" trench, a "cover" trench for the supports, and communication trenches; for this purpose he

must needs have a fair knowledge of the penetrability of different substances (F.S.P.B., page 82).

4. To supervise the construction of " abatis."

5. To place obstacles and dummy parapets to the best advantage.

He should also have some knowledge of the best method of defending woods, posts, and villages.

SPECIAL TRAINING FOR OFFICERS AND SERGEANTS.

Before commencing Engineering with the company it will be wise to go through the work that is expected of the officers and sergeants, as shewn above, making a class of them. Corporals might be included, but it would be hardly necessary to include lance-corporals or selected privates.

If this is not done, the company course is liable to be a case of the blind leading the blind.

It will not be necessary for the officers and non-commissioned officers to spend valuable time actually digging. The only physical work they need do is to construct headcover of different materials, erect wire entanglements, and tie a few simple knots and lashings.

In this work the only thing to do is to follow the Manual of Field Engineering closely.

What will take more time is the siting of fire trenches to the best advantage, the tracing of them, the placing of support and communication trenches, and obstacles and dummy parapets.

It will be best to take the class to some possible position and then theoretically to put the position in a state of defence, shewing where all the trenches, etc., would be. Then take them out to some other suitable ground and test them in carrying out what they have learnt.

It will be best to divide them up into small parties of two and three, mixing up Officers and non-commissioned officers; give them a limited time for the work in hand, with the object of making them think quickly; then take the whole class over the ground from one flank to the other, and call upon each party in turn to give their opinion as to the defence of the position in that quarter.

In the same way after giving a short lecture on the defence of woods, posts, and villages (F.S.P.B., pages 92, 93), take the class out in the country and show practically how this would be carried out in each case. Time will probably not allow of more than one practice.

Note.—On such occasions as these, when taking a class of Officers and non-commissioned officers some distance into the country *don't waste time walking out;* arrange for a rendezvous, and let everyone get out as best he can.

The Officers and Sergeants should now have a clear idea of what they are supposed to know and should also be able to supervise the men in field engineering.

LECTURE TO OPEN COMPANY COURSE WITH.

This subject is best opened with a lecture in which the following points are emphasized:—

1. The necessity for the infantry man nowadays being as proficient with pick and shovel as with rifle and bayonet.

2. The need for him to be able to work as effectively by night as by day.

3. The need for him to be able rapidly to construct for himself, even when lying down, sufficient bullet-proof cover to protect his person.

4. The fact that whatever the nature or dimensions of the cover, it is no use as cover from fire unless it is bullet-proof.

5. The need for arranging in all cover for the best use of the rifle (viz., so arranging that a man standing fires from a height of about 4 ft. 6 ins. above the ground, kneeling 3 feet).

6. The paramount necessity of completely hiding all work done, in other words making it exactly like the surrounding ground.

Having explained what is called for from the non-commissioned officer and man under the head of Field Engineering, you proceed with the practical work. You have decided that your engineering programme is to include for the company as a whole:—

(1) Entrenching (including the preparatory work of extending as a working party).

(2) Use of the entrenching implement.

(3) Making of traverses and recesses.

(4) Construction of head-cover, loop-holes and overhead cover.

(5) Making of dummy parapets.

(6) Clearance of a foreground and the provision of range marks.

(7) Erection of wire entanglements.

(8) Knotting and lashing.

It should be noticed that whereas (2) to (8) are matters of instruction with practice to follow, (1) is chiefly a physical effort which will need much practice to be able to complete the full task. Consequently it will be necessary, whilst instructing the company in the remaining subjects, to train the men progressively in digging. Of course, it is possible that in a country-raised battalion the men are already adept with the pick and shovel, in which case much time will be saved for other work.

However, in the more usual case of city-raised battalions, few men will have done much with the pick and shovel.

It is well to begin with 1½ hours' digging, then extend it to 2 hours, then 3, then 4. It is wise to train the men to keep up a good average of work all the time ; on Active Service trenches have to be dug " against time " more often than not.

It is unlikely that sufficient picks and shovels will be available for the whole company. Consequently, whilst half the company are entrenching, the other half might be receiving instruction in the making of head-cover, loopholes, or overhead cover.

It is necessary to keep a careful record of the work done by each platoon.

It is a good plan, whenever any work has been completed, to assemble the whole company when convenient (probably at the end of a parade), and to criticise the work done, drawing attention to its good and bad points.

Before doing any digging at all it is wise to get the company trained in the rapid and orderly issue of picks and shovels, and in extending as a working party, both of which should be practised by night as well as by day.

ISSUING PICKS AND SHOVELS.

This may sound a trivial matter, but it is far from it.

It will frequently be necessary on Active Service to issue tools rapidly and silently, especially at night.

Confusion or delay will arise unless some such system as the following is in vogue.

The company is drawn up for entrenching practice, with rifles slung. Arrange for the picks and shovels to be laid out in two long lines, a yard apart, handles inwards.

Let the line of picks start, say 10 yards, after the line of shovels.

March the company in single file between these lines, each man bending down and taking the first tool on either side he comes to; an Officer or non-commissioned officer will see to it that the picks (which will probably number not much more than half the shovels) are fairly distributed throughout the whole line.

The non-commissioned officer leading the line will halt, say 60 yards, beyond the end of the tools, each man taking his place (as in two ranks) as he comes up.

Men must be cautioned when moving with tools (which are carried at the "trail"), or when turning in close order to avoid one tool striking against another.

EXTENSION OF WORKING PARTIES.

To do this expeditiously and without noise by day or night will take a little practice. There are several ways of doing it. The following has been found useful.

*Draw up the company in line, say 40 yards, in rear of the proposed trench, the centre of the company approximating to the centre of the trench. Extend the company from the centre to two paces.

Advance the company thus extended on to the actual line of trench. Halt them. Then, starting at one flank, step off each man's task (normally two paces); each man at once puts his pick into the ground on the left of his task, as marked by you; he then steps back four paces, removes his slung rifle, accoutrements, and coat, and sits down; the rifles should be left within reach from the trench itself.

Directly you arrive at the other flank (it takes practically no time), you blow your whistle and every man starts work on the left of his task.

---

* The Company only is referred to here, but the system applies equally if only a platoon, or even a section, is concerned.

It is found in practice that this system takes very little time learning and is very quickly carried out.

THE ENTRENCHING IMPLEMENT.

Steps should be taken to ensure that during the digging course the whole company get plenty of practice with their own entrenching implements as well as with the ordinary pick and shovel.

Every man should be able to construct quickly with his entrenching implement sufficient cover to protect himself when lying down (M.F.E., Plate 9, Fig. 5). In ordinary soil this should not take more than 10 to 15 minutes.

He should further be practised in doing the same thing when lying down, as that is the position in which he would have to work if the line was held up in the attack and could make no further progress.

COMPETITION IN ENTRENCHING.

It will be found a useful practice to let platoons dig their own trenches unassisted, and to promote competition between them in constructing the best trench in the shortest time; for this purpose it would be necessary to apportion the length of trench to the actual number in the platoon.

DOUBLE MANNING.

Practice should also be given in "double manning" the trench, so that when necessary two men can work effectively on one man's ordinary "task."

IMPROVED TRENCHES.

As progress is made, trenches should be made more complete, with facilities for cooking in the trench, food, water, and ammunition storage, as well as recesses for each man's ammunition (M.F.E., plates 16, 17, 19, and 20).

DRAINAGE AND LATRINES.

Special attention should be paid to the drainage of trenches, and latrines connecting with the trenches should be dug.   These should be planned in the original siting of the trench.

VARIOUS TYPES.

It is a mistake to endeavour to teach many different kinds of trench.   Time is very limited, and it is wisest to confine oneself to certain recognised types which have been evolved during the present war.

It is wise to start with a suitable fire trench, say, 2ft. wide, 3ft. 6in. deep, with a parapet 1ft. high and 4ft. broad (you should always arrange for a man to fire over a height of 4ft. 6in.). You should then conceal it with the sods previously taken off.

Your next trench should be a traversed one (M.F.E., Plate 12). It is good practice, for hasty entrenching work, to mark out the traverses, about 8 to 10 yards apart, but not to cut them till you have completed the rest of the trench; this will give you a series of useful trenches for a few men, which, if time be available, can easily be connected round the traverses.

A parados (M.F.E., Plate 12, Fig. 3) might be built for this trench in addition to the parapet. This is a parapet in rear of the trench, and is useful in case you decide, for purposes of concealment, and where there is good "command," to have no parapet in front, as it gives a background to the head of the firer.

It is also very popular in the present war, in addition to the parapet in front, as a protection from the back kick of German shrapnel; the dimensions are, as a rule, 2ft. high and 2ft. thick at the top. It has, of course, to be carefully concealed.

Your next trench should be traversed and recessed, and have a parados (M.F.E., Plates 12 and 13).

First of all, dig your 2ft. by 3ft. 6in. trench, then recess it, placing recesses about 2ft. 3in. apart.* The recesses should vary from 2ft., to take one man, to 4ft. 9in., to take three men; each should be dug in 18in. and 3ft. 6in. deep.

Then deepen the trench itself to 5ft., and build steps behind one or more of the traverses, to enable the occupants to get out quickly. All that remains is to conceal it, including parapet, parados, the ground in front and rear, and the bottom of the trench itself.

Various types of head cover might later be practised on the parapet of this trench.

It should be pointed out that in such a trench as this the maximum of safety from artillery and rifle fire is secured, as the only

---

*The distance between the recesses depends on the nature of the soil. If crumbly you would have to place the recesses at least 2 ft. 6 ins. apart unless the sides were well revetted.

men that need be occupying the trench are
the firers, who stand in the recesses, and are
further protected by the traverses. The trench
itself becomes practically only a communication trench, though it may be used for supports when required. The disadvantage of
the trench is the very limited amount of fire
that can be delivered from it.

It may be noted here that the elbow rest
has been practically abandoned in the present
campaign.

It used to be considered that in order to
provide against shell fire (which is vastly more
effective in this than in any previous campaign) it was necessary to build overhead
cover over the fire trenches. This idea has
been given up as it was found that overhead
cover hampered the actions of the defenders
in repelling an assault.

Consequently overhead cover has been rele-
gated to the support and communication
trenches where it is absolutely essential.

HEAD COVER AND LOOPHOLES.

When practising head cover and loopholes
(M.F.E., page 27, plates 10 and 11), it is
wise to use several different kinds of material, viz., sods, sandbags, sacks, or boxes

filled with earth or gravel, etc. In this way the men get accustomed to make the best of any material that is available.

The necessity of making the head cover bullet-proof, and also of concealing it as far as possible, should be emphasized.

COMMUNICATION TRENCHES AND COVER TRENCHES.

Besides fire trenches simple forms of communication trenches and cover trenches should be constructed (M.F.E., page 29, and plates 16, 20), if time allows, wide enough to take a stretcher.

Whatever the nature of the entrenchment, never fail to conceal it, before you finish with it, from above, as well as from the front.

CONCEALMENT OF TRENCHES.

Points to emphasize:—

Avoid straight lines, conform to the lay of the ground, keep parapets low (18 inches should be ample except when entrenching on a steep slope), and copy the appearance of the surrounding ground as far as possible. When placing sods on the parapet fit them in carefully; remember that the enemy are searching for your trenches with telescopes and field glasses.

If, owing to the nature of the surrounding ground it is thought advisable to stick in the parapet branches of trees and brush, these must be renewed frequently, as otherwise when they wither they are liable to give away the trench.

When cutting sods on no account take them from ground which might be visible to the enemy.

Whilst the trench is being constructed either go yourself or send an Officer to the enemy's possible gun positions (when such is possible) to ensure invisibility.

Impress upon the company that in any defensive position a single trench that is not properly concealed is liable to give away to the hostile artillery the whole position.

DUMMY PARAPETS.

These can easily be practised when improving the simple fire trench, as there will be much earth to spare (M.F.E., page 25). They are often useful in misleading the enemy.

OBSTACLES.
(M.F.E., pages 35-36.)

Time will probably prevent any obstacles being practised except wire entanglements; these are so universal nowadays that everyone should have a knowledge of their construction, especially the high wire entanglement (M.F.E., page 36). It should be impressed on the company that the main object of all obstacles is not so much to stop the attacking troops as to deflect them into narrow areas where they will come under the concentrated fire of the defenders. Trip wires have also been found very effective in bringing down charging German cavalry.

CLEARANCE OF FOREGROUND AND PROVISION OF RANGE-MARKS.

It should be impressed on all that in any defensive position one of the first objects of one's attention is the field of fire. For, if possible, 200 to 300 yards the field of fire should be perfect. In some cases the field of fire, though not naturally good, can be made so by clearance of foreground.

It is not likely that much time can be spared to practise this, but it will be of great help if, whenever the ground is suitable, the company can be shown how the ground would be cleared to provide a good field of fire, and how range-marks would be erected. (M.F.E., pages 21, 22).

KNOTS AND LASHINGS.

(M.F.E., page 59).

Instruction in this should be confined to wet weather, so that fine weather is not wasted on instruction in quarters or camp.

The first thing to do is to get suitable rope; this should be provided by the authorities.

The next thing to do is to discover the knot tiers of the company. Any men who have been to sea, or have river or lake experience will probably be able to tie the simple knots.

Having discovered a good few non-commissioned officers and men who are proficient, regardless of what platoon they belong to, tell them off as instructors to the company, each man having so many men to instruct. Tell them what knots you wish taught on that parade, and the order they are to be taught in, and let them understand that every man has to be taught those particular knots. Otherwise you will find the experts going on to intricate knots of no particular value.

Arrange that the instructors have the same men to teach on all future occasions.

Test the instruction by going round the various groups and singling out an individual in each; call him aside and test his knowledge (don't waste the time of the others by doing it in front of them). There are two things to avoid :—

(1) Teaching useless knots.
(2) Trying to teach too many knots or lashings at one sitting; one hour is quite long enough at a time.

CHAPTER IX.

OFFICERS AND NON-COMMISSIONED OFFICERS—SPECIAL TRAINING.

Special Training Necessary—Best Method—Responsibility of Officers and Non-Commissioned Officers—Syllabus of the Work—Fire—Method of Instruction—Judging Distance—Description of Targets—Control of Fire—Control of Ammunition.

SPECIAL TRAINING NECESSARY.

Officers and non-commissioned officers will require a special training altogether outside the work of the companies.

They will need it, especially if they have had no previous experience. But they will also need it if they have left the Service for some time. An old Officer or soldier may justifiably reflect that his store of knowledge is great beside that of the raw recruit, but that is no excuse for him relying on his previous knowledge, and not making every effort to bring his knowledge up to date. He should realize that every year since he left the Service has seen changes and new methods, most of which he will naturally be ignorant of.

BEST METHOD OF TRAINING.

The special training of the Officers and non-commissioned officers and selected privates will require fitting in as best it may be.

Far the most satisfactory method is to train them before Company Training. Everyday and all day can then be devoted to the task, for which a carefully compiled syllabus should previously be drawn up. It is far better to have them all together for a short time, if it is only four or five days, than to endeavour to fit it in with Company Training.

In such case as this endeavour to arrange to have all your Officers and non-commissioned officers struck off all duties for this purpose. Nothing is so irritating to a Company Commander as to have Officers and non-commissioned officers taken from him during the time specially devoted to their training.

Whilst this special training is going on, the men of the company might be well employed in progressive route-marching, progressive entrenching (from purely a physical point of view), and in any regimental duties and fatigues required. Arrangements should be made regimentally to furnish a few Officers and non-commissioned officers from other companies to supervise such work.

RESPONSIBILITY OF OFFICERS AND NON-COMMISSIONED OFFICERS.

Before commencing on the work of the syllabus it will be as well to impress upon the class the great responsibility that lies upon them.

The credit of their company, the reputation of their regiment, and even the lives of their men will depend on how they perform their duty in the field.

If this fact is properly appreciated it will not be hard to induce the Officers and non-commissioned officers to undergo willingly a strenuous training to fit themselves for their respective tasks.

SYLLABUS OF THE WORK.

The following subjects should be dealt with : —

FIRE.

Judging Distance
Description of targets.

Directing and controlling fire.
Controlling expenditure of ammunition.

TACTICS.

Eye for ground.
Quick decision.
Initiative.
Keeping direction.

RECONNAISSANCE.

Messages and reports.
Map Reading.
Finding way by sun and stars.
Compass (Officers only).

The engineering knowledge required of Officers and non-commissioned officers has already been dealt with on pages 93-94.

Besides the above all the Officers and a fair proportion of non-commissioned officers should be trained in the use of the range finder.

We will now consider the various headings:—

FIRE.

METHOD OF INSTRUCTION.

The best system is to take the class out—on each occasion to different ground—and to practise them in the various subjects under this head.

First of all, with the class lying down as if in the attack, give a practical illustration yourself in " Fire Direction and Control," viz·: Call out, " I see through glasses some of the enemy's trenches in the middle of the grass field just to the left of the field with the big trees in the hedge.   I want fire brought to bear on those trenches as quickly as possible.   *Section—half right—at the middle of the grass field immediately to the left of the field with the big trees in the hedge—850—fire."

Bending down, you then run a few paces first towards one flank and then the other, to observe whether every man is firing at the correct object and whether his sights appear to be correctly adjusted (the Platoon or Section Commander will always know the likely offenders and pay attention chiefly to them).

This movement behind the men firing is of course only practicable at the longer ranges; at the shorter ranges all you could do would be to enquire down the line whether everyone had got the right target and correct sighting.

---

* Some Officers prefer to give the range always first, as it saves the man taking his eye off the target.

It is as well not only to train the Fire Unit Commander to shout the fire orders, but also the men themselves to pass them down.

This will give an idea of what is wanted. You then put the members of the class through the same work, starting with the Officers. Picture a situation every time and let the Officer or non-commissioned officer bring fire to bear as rapidly as possible. When you have done this for half an hour or so noting on paper each time any particular weaknesses, viz.: one man being slow, another bad at judging distance, and another unable to describe his target, then proceed either to a judging distance practice or a description of targets practice. Next time carry on with the class on different ground, beginning from the Officer or non-commissioned officer who was last tested.

Before long you will be able to divide the class up—so many weak at judging distance, so many at description, so many at controlling fire and supervising their men. When you have arrived at this, let each lot work separately at their respective weaknesses.

Certain officers and non-commissioned officers will have passed muster in all branches, and can help you supervising the remainder

Whatever other weakness presents itself, a failure in judging distance is one which absolutely must be corrected; special attention should be paid to the longer ranges, viz., from 800 to 1,400 yards.

In practising description of targets the class should be instructed in the "Finger and Clock" method (Musk. Regs., Part I., Para. 279), but they should only be encouraged to use this method when the range is a long one, and the actual target is invisible to the naked eye.

The landscape targets will be found a very useful help in instructing the class in this subject.

CHAPTER X.

OFFICERS AND NON-COMMISSIONED OFFICERS.—TACTICS.

Object to be Aimed At—Method of Instruction—
Simple Tactical Schemes—Private Practice—
Discussion Encouraged—Solution of Problems.

OBJECT TO BE AIMED AT.

The object to be aimed at in instruction
in this subject is that each member of the
class should train himself quickly to grasp
any situation that may arise in the field, that
he should decide rapidly and fairly sensibly
what action to take, and finally should shew
initiative by carrying out in a practical way
what he has decided to do.

A good deal of practice will be required.
Some men have a natural aptitude for such
work as this; others start indifferently, but
improve rapidly with practice. Those who
become proficient quickly can well be utilised
to help instruct the weaker ones.

METHOD OF INSTRUCTION.

A good method of instruction is as follows :
Take the class out, if possible, to new ground. As they are marching out, suddenly halt them, and exclaim : " A half-company of the enemy are in the edge of that wood firing on you. What are you going to do?" That makes every man *think quickly*, which is half the battle. You call on some individual to give his opinion, then, without commenting on it, you call on another and then possibly a third. You then criticise the various suggestions, and give them your opinion.

When you have got to the ground you are making for, picture a situation which involves driving the enemy out of a position ; put it to the class " How are you going to attack?" Assume that they have their normal command, a platoon, or section, as the case may be.

At the end of five minutes, call upon different officers and men to give their views ; occasionally ask another of the same rank to criticise the view expressed.

SIMPLE TACTICAL SCHEMES.

Another good practice is to take them on to some rising ground and to give them 15 minutes to put (theoretically) a certain portion of it in a state of defence. In such a practice as this it is often best to divide them up into small syndicates of three or four, each syndicate containing seniors and juniors; at the end of half an hour assemble the class and call upon a few of the syndicates to give their views. Let them select their own spokesman; if, however, the syndicates are set other problems, always ask another member to give the views of the syndicate on the next occasion.

In the same way small Retirement schemes and Protection schemes can be worked; in the case of the former the class would be called upon to suggest the successive fire-positions that would be taken up by troops retiring; in the case of the latter the position of the piquets and sentry groups might be the test.

To afford the best instruction in all such schemes as these it is essential that the Company Commander should have been over the ground before, if possible with a companion, and thought out the solution to the various problems he is going to set. If he is unable to do this, the instruction he gives is bound to suffer from being thought out on the spur of the moment. This is unfortunate in itself, but its effect may be even worse, as it is liable to impair the confidence the company should have in their commander.

The result of these schemes is very quickly noticeable. A much quicker grasp of the situation is soon manifested, and initiative displayed by men whom one had previously thought to be totally lacking in it.

There is one point that applies to all these schemes. Never give the officer or non-commissioned officer a theoretical command which he is not likely to exercise—viz., there is no good purpose served in giving a subaltern command of a battalion, nor a corporal that of a company.

PRIVATE PRACTICE.

It will be found of great benefit if you can encourage your Officers and non-commissioned officers to practise this kind of " study of ground " whenever in the country on duty or pleasure.

All they have to do is to picture some simple situation ; viz., let them picture to themselves that their company is acting as Advanced Guard to the Battalion moving along the road that they are on at the time.

Suddenly the Advance Party are fired on from a line of trees parallel to the road 500 yards half right. Let them make up their minds quickly what action they (as Officer Commanding Company) would take, and what message they would send back to the Commanding Officer. This particular scheme is intended for officers; similar ones for non-commissioned officers can easily be suggested.

Even if they are alone and have no one to consult, the value of the practice in rapid grasp of the situation and encouragement of initiative cannot well be exaggerated. If they have a companion with them, the exchange of views will make it even more useful.

DISCUSSION ENCOURAGED.

It is also a good thing to encourage the members of the class to discuss the various situations and the various solutions on the way home and when they get back to their quarters; this induces them to look at tactics as a subject of absorbing interest instead of as dry matter intended purely for senior officers.

I 2

SOLUTION OF PROBLEMS.

In the matter of the opinions you give, it is most necessary to point out to the class that there is no such thing as *the correct solution* of a tactical problem.

Of every problem there are probably two or three solutions that are equally sound. Just because one of the class suggests a different solution to the one that you have selected, it by no means implies that he is wrong. If he supports his solution with reasonably sound arguments, it should be accepted as a good one.

Your chief task is to draw attention to any points in the various solutions that show lack of common sense or offend against any recognised rules of tactics.

In doing this, avoid excessive diffidence. Some officers are so disinclined to " lay down the law " in matters of tactics, that they give the impression that almost any solution may be right. Such an officer is likely to get the reputation of not knowing his own mind; this is fatal to that confidence which it is essential that a good Company Commander should inspire in his men.

KEEPING DIRECTION.

It may happen at any time that an officer or non-commissioned officer is required to act as guide to the company either in drill or on manœuvre.

In the attack, for instance, it is of vital importance that the correct direction should be maintained; the slightest deviation from it may throw the attack out.

Consequently it is essential that all officers and non-commissioned officers should be able to act as guide to the company.

The guide must not be fettered with any other duty nor must his attention be distracted for a moment. He should be taught always to take two points to march on, the more clearly defined the better. As he approaches the nearer one, he should take another one further off but in line and so on.

A rapid method of instruction is as follows:—Take the class on to some high ground, if possible, with extensive view in most directions.

Put a stick into the ground; make one of the class stand with his back to the stick and tell him to march on some point in the distance, a side of a house, a tall tree, etc.

Directly he has started, do the same with another man but not quite in the same direction, and so on until you have about six men marching on points radiating from you.

Instruct them that when they have gone about 400 to 500 yards to march back, taking you as the point to march on. It is wise to have a non-commissioned officer to assist you in watching the men and making note of any lapses from the direct line. When the men have all returned draw their attention to any errors, and send out another party.

Any who show weakness must be given further practice. Whilst you are supervising half the class, your second-in-command might be supervising the other half. It is sometimes assumed that an officer can guide a company without practice; it is a most unwise assumption.

Note:—When selecting points for the men to march on, the more broken the ground the better; it is also excellent practice if the man has to dip down into a hollow during his march, but he should be visible to the centre point for most of the distance.

CHAPTER XI.

OFFICERS AND NON-COMMISSIONED OFFICERS—RECONNAISSANCE.

Scope of Subject—Field Messages—Method of Instruction—Sample Field Message—Essential Points—Reports—Map Reading—Objects Aimed At—Finding One's Way by the North Point—Compass for Officers.

Under the heading of Reconnaissance we will for the present purpose include:—Messages and Reports, Map Reading, Ability to find one's way by the north point, Compass (time will only permit the instruction of officers in this).

There are, of course, many other subjects which might come under this heading and which might be taught if time were ample, but for the present purpose we must stick to essentials.

MESSAGES AND REPORTS.

(F.S.R., Part I., pages 22, 35, 36).

It is incumbent on all officers and non-commissioned officers that they should be able to write a good field message and a clear and concise report. General rules regarding the preparation and despatch of these will be found in Field Service Regulations as quoted above.

METHOD OF INSTRUCTION.

The whole class must be provided with pocket-books and pencils. It is wise to issue to each non-commissioned officer a sample pocket-book of handy size (to go in the breast pocket). The officers will, of course, have their own. (Note: Indelible pencils are not recommended; they are troublesome in wet weather.) The first thing to do is to give them an example of an ordinary field message, on a black-board, if possible, viz:—

Col. SMITH, Comdg. Adv. Gd.,
> BLUE Force.

>> Head of Main Guard.

No. 2*, Sept. 3rd. On arrival here I was heavily fired on from wood 600 yds. on my right. Unable at present to give strength of enemy, but I have sent scouts to find out.

> A. JONES, SERGT.,
>> i/c Advance Party,
800 yds. W. of UPTON CHURCH,
>> 11.30 a.m.

---

* Refers to the number of messages you have despatched during that day regardless of whom they were sent to.

As regards this message, it is not essential to put in the addressee's name; O.C. Adv. Gd. would do equally well.

As regards his address, you do not know where the Main Guard will be at the moment, so you are unable to put the name of a place. In his Advanced Guard orders the Officer Commanding would have stated that his position would be at the head of the Main Guard; (it might equally well be with the Support of the Van Guard). Some non-commissioned

officers have a tendency to put their name
and rank at the end, but to omit what their
job is, which, of course, is the important
thing.

You then proceed to picture a situation to
them which involves their writing a field
message. They have to give the necessary information in their field message
as concisely and clearly as possible.
Plenty of time should be allowed to start
with, a process of speeding up taking place
at each subsequent practice. You would go
over their messages in your spare time and
criticise them individually at the next
parade; your officers should assist you in this
work.

The following points should be drawn
attention to:—

1. The overwhelming importance of clear
   writing; an illegible message is often
   worse than useless.

2. The inserting at the end of the message
   of the time you despatched it, and as
   far as possible the place you send it
   from; don't put simply the name of a
   neighbouring village, but rather "500
   yards west of UPTON WINDMILL."

3. Be most careful about stops; they are liable to alter the whole sense.

4. When finished writing and checking, if possible give it to a companion to read (selecting a stupid one for preference). If he can understand it, it will probably convey the information desired to the recipient.

   Note.—It is obvious that this could not be done in case of urgency, but even in that case, never omit to check what you have written.

5. Avoid the natural tendency to report in vague terms, viz.—"A 'large' number of the enemy,"—this is utterly vague and misleading. Rather say, for instance, "A body of the enemy which looks about a company strong." You may not be right as to their numbers, but such a description is better than using indefinite terms.

6. It should be pointed out that in the field it would be criminal in case of urgency for an officer or non-commissioned officer to waste time trying to recollect the exact form of a cor-

rect field message. Let him make sure of four things:—

(1) That it is legible.
(2) That it conveys his meaning.
(3) That it is timed.
(4) That it is clearly addressed and signed.

You would then carry out a similar practice in the field, picturing a situation to the class when they were not prepared for it, and then letting them compete (in their own ranks) in dashing off a good field message against time.

REPORTS.

This subject is concisely dealt with in F.S.R., Part I., page 36.

It may not be out of place here to emphasize the vital importance of negative reports. It may frequently happen that it is as important to know that the enemy are not in a certain place at a certain time as to know that they are.

MAP READING.

It is most necessary to be very clear about the amount of instruction needed in this

subject. Little time is available, and therefore the instruction must be condensed as far
as possible.

The object should be for all officers and
non-commissioned officers to be " handy with
a map," i.e., whatever the scale, to be able
to estimate distances on it quickly. They
should, without measuring, be able to give
fairly accurately the number of miles between any places. They should learn the
different methods of representing heights,
and the officers and sergeants should be able
to read and understand contours; it is not
necessary for them to be able to draw them.
They should be quick in spotting the rivers.

They should be able to " set a map," either
by " objects " or by compass (F.S.P.B.,
pages 77, 78).

Officers should be able to enlarge a map.

No attempt whatever should be made to
teach the construction of scales; time is too
valuable for that.

It is a good practice to get them to be
constantly studying maps, and if maps of the
same country, but of different scales, are
obtainable the practice is so much the more
useful.

It will be found useful to combine questions of time and distance with map reading

—viz., picture a simple situation on a large scale map—say an Advanced Guard scheme with a company acting as Advanced Guard to a battalion. The Main Guard is at a certain point on the road at 10 a.m. Where will the head of the Main Body be at 12.30 p.m. ?

The pace of other arms should also be represented to the class by distance travelled on the map.

They should have a fair knowledge of the ordinary Conventional Signs.

FINDING ONE'S WAY BY THE NORTH POINT.

The class should be instructed in the watch hand method for day observation, and in the position of the Pole star for night work. (F.S.P.B., pages 78, 79.)

COMPASS.

(F.S.P.B., page 78.)

Officers should be able to use the ordinary Service compass by day or night.

They should be practised in marching on a compass bearing night and day, so that they could lead a night advance, or could guide the company in the attack by compass bearing by day.

CHAPTER XII.

AIRCRAFT AND INFANTRY, Etc.

Aircraft and Infantry—Training of Scouts—
Training in Night Operations—The Moral
Factor.

It is as well to impress upon the company
the meaning of the advent of aircraft into
modern war.

The present war has already in a few
months given an inkling of what the future
has in store for us.

Points to emphasize.

1. Distinction between the heavier than
   air machines, viz., aeroplanes,
   including monoplanes, biplanes, sea-
   planes, and the lighter than air
   vessels—airships and balloons.

2. The former have already proved themselves. Airships, on the other hand,
   are at the present moment still experi-
   mental owing to their being so depen-
   dent on the elements, easily destroyed

by storm, helpless on the ground
except in a special shed, and affording
a good target for hostile guns and
rifles. On the other hand they have
a much wider range of action and infi-
nite capacity for doing harm—for
instance, they can carry four or five
tons of explosives.

Aeroplanes have already justified their
existence in the following rôles:—

(1) *Strategic Reconnaissance.*—They have
flown right behind the enemy's first
line.

(2) *Tactical Reconnaissance.*—They have
kept their forces informed of any
important movement of troops from
one part of the battle ground to
another.

(3) *Direction of Artillery Fire.*—They
have located the enemy's trenches and
their guns again and again, and succeeded, by dropping smoke bombs or
signalling in other ways, in enabling
their own artillery to find the range
exactly. They have also assisted the
naval guns on board the Monitors
lying off the coast of Belgium near
Ostend, to shell the German trenches.

(4) *Dropping Bombs.*—So far the effect of
dropping bombs has been chiefly
moral, but it must be remembered
that the bombs carried by an airship
are vastly more dangerous than the
lighter variety carried by the aeroplane. Some British naval airmen
paid two visits to Dusseldorf on the
Rhine, and on the second occasion are
supposed to have caused very serious
damage to a Zeppelin airship.

The energy of the aircraft on either side
has been so great as to lead to many duels in
the air, in which skill in manœuvring, cool-
ness, and accurate revolver shooting have
been the features.

The immediate questions for us as infantry
men are:—

1. How can we avoid the airman seeing
   us and our trenches?
2. How can we bring him down?

1. Cover from Aircraft.

It is too much to expect that we can avoid
him detecting our trenches, though much can
be done by well concealed overhead cover.

If, however, troops are in the open, much
can be done to avoid detection; the following
rules will be found useful:—

R. T.   K

(1) Don't move about—stand still or lie
down.

(2) Don't look up at the aircraft; that is
fatal.

(3) If on the march and an aircraft
approaches, keep to the sides of the
road; if the road is lined with trees
or hedges they give excellent cover.

The fact that hostile aircraft are in observation must not, however, cause interference
with the Commander's plans. For instance,
it may be more needful to move troops
rapidly from one point to another and to
risk being spotted rather than for the troops
to spend valuable time hiding from aircraft.

Again, if an attack is in progress, no effort
must be made by the attacking troops to
seek cover from aircraft.

2. How to bring the Airman down.

Experience in the present war will no doubt
show us later what are the best means of
attacking aircraft, whether it be one attacking the other, anti-aircraft guns and shrapnel
fire, machine-gun fire, or concentrated rifle
fire. The only one that immediately con-
cerns us, however, is the last.

From a rifleman's point of view damaging aircraft is a very difficult matter. Airships are a better target and much more vulnerable than aeroplanes, but as both types of aircraft are liable to be travelling at speeds up to 50 miles an hour, and are likely to be at least 3,000 feet up, the chances of a rifle bullet damaging them is not very great.

In the case, too, of aeroplanes bullets can pass through the wings without doing serious damage.

Indiscriminate fire at hostile aircraft is, moreover, likely to cause casualties in neighbouring units, and will also disclose the troops to the aircraft observer.

Consequently fire directed at aircraft must be strictly controlled. Men should be instructed to fire in front of the aeroplane six times the length of the machine, and at the nose of the envelope in the case of the airship.

TRAINING OF SCOUTS.

In the short time available this is a difficult matter. There can be little doubt that under the circumstances it will be best not to attempt to train them in the company. The most effective way will be for each company to recommend its five most suitable men and one non-commissioned officer, all of whom should be not only volunteers for the work, but enthusiasts.

A great deal will depend on getting suitable men for the work of scouts. To ensure this, it is wise to emphasize the importance of the work, the tribute accorded to the worth of a man by being selected as a scout, and further in every way to demonstrate that the company scouts are the picked men of the company. They should also be excused all guard duties, and the customary duties and fatigues as far as possible.

This party should then be trained regimentally by an officer (two if they can be spared) with a sergeant to assist, specially selected for the duty. After a week or so the officer in charge would be able to " return to duty " the most unlikely man of each company, thus leaving four scouts per company. Even then the number will be large, but the instruction given will probably be a good deal better than it would be by endeavouring to train them in the companies.

Their training should, if possible, be carried out when Company Training is not on ; if, however, that is not practicable, they should do their Company Training with their companies with the exception of parades from which they could be spared, viz., the early morning parade, which is devoted as a rule to close order drill or physical exercises, and a proportion of route-marches; the time saved in this way added to work in the evenings would enable them to get a certain amount of training. Whenever the Company work needed scouts they would fulfil the duty, thereby gaining useful experience.

The actual subjects for training the scout in and the qualifications required are concisely shewn in Infantry Training (1914), page 112.

TRAINING IN NIGHT OPERATIONS.

(I.T., Sec. 113).

An early opportunity in the training should be taken to impress upon the company the fact that recent wars, and especially the present one, have made night work almost as important as day work. Again and again troops have had to wait till dark before they could make any real progress; night attacks, too, by the Germans on the Allies' trenches have been the rule rather than the exception in the operations north of the Aisne (October, 1914).

It therefore becomes a matter of vital importance that troops should be able to march, attack, dig, hold a position, or retire, by night as well as by day.

Considerable training also will be required to improve their sight and hearing in the dark, and further to teach them to move noiselessly.

The detail of the training suggested will be found in the above quoted paragraph (Infantry Training).

If the time of the year permits, it is advisable to do the night work early in the evening after dark.

It will thus not interfere to any extent with the ordinary programme of work. In the summer, however, night operations cannot take place till late in the evening. On such occasions it is advisable to curtail the following morning's work.

THE MORAL FACTOR.

It is not difficult to imagine what "the man in the street," in a neutral country, who is unprejudiced, if such can now be found, would say about our present great efforts to fashion armies.

As to our Regular Army he would, no doubt, say "Small, but very good." He would have in mind its history, its traditions, earned in the Peninsula, at Waterloo, and in the battles of the Crimea, and he would frankly admit that the retreat from Mons and the operations on the Aisne proved that the officers and men of to-day were at least worthy of their forbears. But he would say "What of these vast new armies we hear of?" How can they be created in the twinkling of an eye? How can men who were civilians yesterday call themselves soldiers to-day?

The question is a fair one and it is up to us to find an answer.

We must bear in mind that in the new armies that we are forming whether they be composed of the new Regular Battalions, the Oversea Forces, or the Territorial Force, a certain small percentage will be men of previous experience either in peace or war, but the vast majority will either be new to the work altogether, or will have only had a week or two's training a year for at most eight or ten years.

Yet in the space of a few months we hope to place these troops in the field and pit them against the best fighting machine in the world.

How are we to do it?

We are here only concerned with the Infantry. In previous pages we have endeavoured to show how best to utilise, as far as Company Training is concerned, the brief time available in thorough, systematic, and intelligent training.

But, considering the goal which we are aiming at, the lack of competent instructors, and the need for haste, we should feel more than doubtful about success, were it not for one thing:—

" The moral is to the physical as 3 to 1."

The words are Napoleon's, and worthy of the speaker.

We know well what can be done in a short time with raw material, by giving them the best training, in the time of peace. We know, further, that far greater results are possible under the stimulus of war.

But we do not know what can be done when the manhood of an empire, of its own free will, flies to arms in defence of that empire and of the causes that it holds most dear. Is it too much to hope that the work of years in peace time can be accomplished in as many months in war time?

The rapid rise in recruiting which has taken place during the present war, when our arms have met with a set-back, together with the splendid response of the Dominions, have proved that the old Latin motto which served as an incentive to the Roman soldier is equally the sentiment of the Britisher to-day: "Dulce et decorum est pro patriâ mori."

We know further that every soldier in the ranks is imbued with determination to learn his job as effectually as possible; he grudges neither time, discomfort, nor the restriction of discipline. With such material, and such spirit, much is possible.

The rest depends chiefly on the officer and non-commissioned officer. Theirs is a tremendous task. May they prove equal to it!

We may take comfort to ourselves in the reflection that the experience of the present war has put a greater strain on the moral qualities of the soldier than it has, if possible, on the physical.

When one realises what our troops have had to undergo, whether it be in the ceaseless fighting, with no rest, in the Mons retreat, or the hardships since involved in days together in the trenches, often in the worst of weather, we appreciate the truth of Napoleon's remark quoted above.

We have no reason to doubt that the new armies will display the same constancy and the same fortitude.

No doubt the above pages will reach many whose chance of service at the front seems, at the present time, small. Their task, though less attractive, is equally valuable service to the Empire.

None know when their chance may come, and if it does come, and they have not taken the opportunity of their increased training time to become thoroughly efficient, there are few who would envy their feelings.

That, however, is a contingency of which there are certainly no signs visible.

APPENDIX I.

CUSTOMS OF THE SERVICE.

Though the subject of this title can hardly be considered part of Company Training, at the same time it may not be out of place, under present circumstances, to offer a few suggestions on a question which frequently exercises greatly the minds of Officers who have had little military experience.

OFFICERS' MESS.

Firstly, as regards the Mess :—

The Mess should be looked upon as a home, and the members of it should regard each other as brother officers in fact as well as in name.

If that is the case, there will be no exaggerated deference paid to rank whilst in the Mess.*

When on parade, " Sir " and saluting must be the rule; when off parade, friendly terms and nicknames are the best means of pro-

---

*In several regiments it is the rule for mess kit to carry no badges of rank ; this emphasizes the brother-officer idea.

ducing a real regimental spirit among the Officers. The only persons who should be addressed by their rank are the Colonel and Majors.

The Colonel on all occasions should be treated with deference, and always addressed as " Sir."

Mess dinner, even in war time, should be regarded as a parade, and punctuality insisted on.

On arriving in the Mess in the morning it is customary to wish the senior officer present " Good morning," and on arrival in the Mess before dinner to wish the senior officer " Good evening." When the Commanding Officer comes into the Ante-Room before dinner the officers present should rise and wish him " Good evening."

Bad language and risqué stories are taboo in a good Mess : they are the hall-mark of a bad one.

Young Officers on joining should regard themselves as on probation ; they should take note of everything, be inclined to keep in the background, and even if they feel to know more about a subject under discussion than those taking part in it, are well advised

not to air their views at too early a stage in
their military career.

TREATING.

It is a fatal mistake to allow "treating"
in either an Officers' or Sergeants' Mess.
Whenever a Mess gets a bad name for intem-
perance, it can nearly always be traced to
neglect of this rule. To take a concrete instance. A young subaltern is playing bridge
in a Mess where there is no such rule. After
a time he feels desirous of a "drink." He
cannot well order one without offering one to
his three companions. Suppose they all accept, the subaltern has to pay for four drinks
instead of one, and the remaining three
Officers feel in duty bound to stand drinks
each in turn. Result: The subaltern can
hardly escape paying for four times as much
drink as he wants or can afford, and con-
sumes four times as much as is good for him.

On the other hand, when the salutary rule
exists as to "non-treating," and *is strictly
carried out*, an Officer orders a drink if he
wants one, and does so without any qualms as
to his reputation for "open-handedness."

CARDS.

It is a sound rule to restrict round games,
such as poker, etc., to guest nights, and then

only for small points, which should be laid down by the Commanding Officer.

If such games are played daily, the same result invariably happens—that some unwise Subaltern quickly runs into debt, and complications ensue.

SALUTING.

When saluting, Officers should stand to attention and salute smartly; a sloppy salute is a painful sight.

Officers should salute their Commanding Officer or 2nd in command whenever met. They should also salute senior Officers of the Staff or other units; it is not necessary to salute other Officers when casually met.

Never fail to return the salute of a non-commissioned officer or private; return it properly, bringing the hand to the forehead. When several Officers are walking together, one may notice that salutes are not always returned. This is generally because either the senior Officers are in doubt as to which is senior (as may happen when Officers of different units are together), or because the senior Officer does not see the salute and the others do not like to take it upon themselves to act as the senior.

Neither of these reasons is anything like sufficient excuse for not returning a salute; it matters but little who does it, but it is most important that it should be done.

PARADE.

Never keep men waiting on parade.

Some Officers think that if the parade is theirs (viz., a subaltern—a platoon parade) they can come on parade five minutes late. This is quite wrong, and bad for discipline.

Before marching off a party always ask permission of the senior Officer, whether of your own or of another corps, on parade.

OFFICIAL REBUKES.

Do not let official "tellings off" affect personal relations.

In a good regiment, an Adjutant may give a thorough "dressing down" to a junior in the morning, and yet in the afternoon be enjoying a long walk or ride with him.

DRESS.

Officers should be scrupulous about their appearance. Shaving before early morning parade is a necessity. Long hair is most unmilitary. Shoes instead of boots are wrong, and fancy socks are an abomination. Great coats should always be "done up" and buttons scrupulously clean.

There is no room for individuality in uniform.

Trousers should never be worn on parade or on duty. They are frequently known as "slacks," which sufficiently indicates their sphere.

APPENDIX II.

*LICE IN WAR.

This subject is an important one for all Officers, Non-Commissioned Officers and men proceeding to the front. There are many discomforts regarded as inseparable from active service. If, however, any can be got rid of altogether, or even mitigated by steps taken before going on service, it is clearly our duty to take them. This is undoubtedly the case with lice. A little knowledge concerning their habits and the necessary steps to combat them may save great discomfort, and possibly serious illness on service.

There are two kinds of lice that concern us :—

    (1) The head louse.

    (2) The body louse.

---

* See Article "Insects and War" by Dr. A. E. Shipley, Sc. D., F.R.S., Master of Christ's College, Cambridge. "British Medical Journal," September 19th, 1914.

We will consider the head louse, which is the less important, first.

THE HEAD LOUSE.

This insect lives in the hair of people who neglect their heads (a frequent case on active service). The egg is cemented to the base of the hair, and at the end of six days hatches out, and becomes mature on the eighteenth day. Many African natives are in the habit of plastering their hair with coloured clay or anointing it with ointment; this would be a protective against the head louse.

On the other hand in some armies, the German among them, the men have their hair very closely cropped, almost shaven. This also would avoid a breeding ground for the insect. The effect the head louse produces is to cause much irritation and skin trouble.

It has also been known to convey certain forms of recurrent fever. It spreads very quickly from man to man.

THE BODY LOUSE.

The body louse is a more serious enemy to deal with, as he is more difficult both to avoid and to get rid of. He lives in under-clothing on the side next the skin. He sucks the blood of his host at least twice a day, and when feeding is almost anchored in the clothes by the claws of one or more of his six legs.

A female will lay an average of five eggs every twenty-four hours; the eggs will hatch out in anything from eight to forty days after they are laid; and the insect has a life of from three to four weeks.

Their continued existence depends, how-ever, on regular food. They not only cause constant irritation, prevent sleep, and weaken the host, but undoubtedly convey most serious diseases, including typhus. They spread very rapidly from man to man; thus men who are perfectly clean in their persons and clothes may get them from men with whom they are in contact.

They are the constant accompaniment of all armies. During the South African War the custom in some regiments was as follows: —Whenever they halted, everyone stripped to the skin, turned their clothes inside out, and picked the insects off. As a private was heard to remark: " We strips and we picks

'em off and places 'em in the sun, and it kind
of breaks the little beggars' 'earts."

Rules.

The following rules have been drawn up
by Dr. A. E. Shipley, who has made a study
of these insects.

It is obvious that many of these rules will,
under the conditions of modern warfare, be
impracticable save on occasions. The idea,
however, is to get everyone to bear these
rules in mind, and act on them whenever the
opportunity offers. An Officer who went
through the whole of the South African War
has borne testimony to the fact that, owing
to carrying them out, he escaped entirely the
presence of lice on his body, and that he was
the only Officer or man in his regiment who
did escape.

1. Avoid sleeping, if possible, where others,
especially the unclean, have slept before—a
good reason for avoiding old camping grounds.

2. Search your person as often as possible
for signs of the bites. When discovered take
the following measures:—

3. Change your clothing as often as possible; after clothes have been left off for a week the lice are usually dead of starvation. Change clothes at night if possible, and place your clothing away from that of the others. Infested clothing and blankets should be placed apart as far as possible.

4. All infested clothing discarded for good should be burnt or buried, or put under water. Socks are not so important as body clothing, as lice rarely affect the forearm, the hands, or the feet. Cholera belts were, in many cases in South Africa, discarded early, owing to infestation of lice.

5. The body louse can be killed as follows: Underclothes may be scalded, say, once in ten days. Turn coats, waistcoats, trousers, etc., *inside out*, examine beneath the folds at the seams, and expose these places to as much heat as can be borne before a fire, against a boiler, or allow a jet of steam from a kettle or boiler to travel over the clothing, especially along the seams. The clothing will soon dry. Petrol and paraffin and sulphur will also kill nits and lice in clothing.

6. The head louse may be destroyed by the application of either petrol, paraffin oil,

turpentine or benzine to the head. This application should be repeated on one or two more days if the head is heavily infested. Fine combs are also useful in removing vermin from the head.

7. As far as possible avoid scratching the irritated part.

MISCELLANEOUS (contd.)

To find true if variation is E., add the degrees.

To find magnetic if variation is W., add the degrees.

To find magnetic if variation is E., subtract the degrees.

PLACING A POSITION IN A STATE OF DEFENCE.

Steps in order of importance :—

1. Dig necessary fire trenches and cover trenches.
2. Improve field of fire.
3. Erect obstacles.
4. Improve communication, and dig communicating trenches.

AIMING OFF FOR MOVEMENT.

Up to 500 yards aim should be taken about :—

1 ft. in front per 100 yards at a single man walking.

2 ft. in front per 100 yards at a single man doubling.

3 ft. in front per 100 yards at a single horseman trotting.

4 ft. in front per 100 yards at a single horseman galloping.

Six times the length of machine in front of an aeroplane.

The nose of the envelope as regards an airship.

FIELD MESSAGE.

O.C. Main Body,
Red Force,
BEDFORD.

No. 4. Oct. 30th ....

....

A. Smith,
Capt.,
Comdg. Adv. Gd.
Red Force,
800x, N. of ELTHAM Rly.
Station.
8.45 a.m.

VERBAL MESSAGE.

To O.C. A Company.

....

....

From Sergt. JONES
Commanding No. 4 Section.
10.30 a.m.

REFERENCE CARD.

OUTPOSTS.

OUTPOST COMPANY COMMANDER.

1. Halt company in rear of ground allotted, with screen of scouts well to the front.

2. Walk over ground allotted, carefully noting features.

3. Decide on the number and position of piquets, supports, and detached posts if needed.

4. Tell off company accordingly, keeping platoons as intact as possible; tell off two outpost patrols.

5. Before company separate instruct them—
   (a) What to do in case of attack.
   (b) What friendly cavalry there are to the front.
   (c) Probable direction of enemy.
   (d) Special arrangements for night.
   (e) Special rules as to smoking, lighting fires, cooking.
   (f) Hour of relief of outposts.
   (g) Your own position.

6. Confidentially tell platoon commanders the private signal, if any.

7. Despatch various platoons to their respective tasks.

8. Communicate with companies on either flank, ensuring that all ground is watched.

9. Visit the sentries.

10. After piquets are entrenched, call in the scouts.

PIQUET COMMANDER.

1. Explain your orders to your piquet.

2. Satisfy yourself that every man knows—
   (a) Direction of the enemy.
   (b) Position of next piquets, and of support, and of any detached post near.
   (c) What to do in case of attack.
   (d) Whether there is any friendly cavalry to the front.

3. Select best position for defence.

4. Trace line of trench and start section digging at once.

5. Walk over ground allotted and decide number and position of sentry posts needed.

6. Tell off necessary groups.

7. Post groups, allotting the front to be watched in each case, and telling sentry group commander what to do with persons trying to enter or leave outpost line.

8. Communicate with piquets on the right and left and ensure all ground being watched.

9. Return to piquet and tell off a sentry over piquet (and two reliefs).

10. Make necessary arrangements for cooking, latrine, and supply of water and ammunition.

SENTRY-GROUP COMMANDER.

1. Tell off the sentries.
2. See that sentries know
(a) Direction of enemy.
(b) Positions of sentries on either side.
(c) Position of piquet, and nearest way to it.
(d) Position of support and of next piquets, and of any detached post in neighbourhood.
(e) What to do in case of attack.

(f) Whether there are any friendly cavalry to the front.
(g) Exact limits of ground they have to watch.
(h) How to deal with persons approaching their post.
(i) Names of all villages, rivers, etc., in view, and where any roads or railways lead to.
(k) Private signal, if there is one.

3. See that sentry can see well without being seen.

ADVANCED GUARD COMMANDER.

(One company acting as Advanced Guard.)

1. Explain task to company, and state your position.
2. Tell off company into Van Guard and Main Guard.
3. Instruct respective commanders of Van Guard and Main Guard to tell off their commands, viz.: Van Guard into Advance Party and Support; Main Guard, sufficient connecting files to keep connection with Main Body.
4. Instruct the two commanders respectively what distance to keep.

5. Despatch various portions in such time as to ensure their all being in position by the time the Main Body is due to start. (Calculate on 3 miles an hour pace, or 100 yards to the minute.)

6. When started, test the company by having messages and signals passed from front to rear.

REAR GUARD COMMANDER.

(One company acting as Rear Guard.)

1. Explain task to the company and state your position.

2. Tell off the company into Rear Party and Main Guard.

3. Instruct whole Guard to turn about whenever they halt.

4. Instruct respective commanders to tell off their commands, viz.: Rear Party into Point and Flankers with connecting files; Main Guard, sufficient connecting files to connect with Main Body.

5. Instruct respective commanders what distance to keep.

FINDING TRUE NORTH.

SUN AND WATCH METHOD:
NORTHERN HEMISPHERE.

Hold watch horizontally. Point the hour hand at the sun. Then a line from centre of dial to a point halfway between figure XII and the pointer of hour hand is approximately a south line.

VARIATION OF THE COMPASS.

England and Ireland—
Varies from 21° W. (West Coast of Ireland) to 15° W. (Kent Coast).
France—
Varies from 15° W. to 12° W.
Germany—
Varies from 12° W. to 5° W.
Canada—
Varies from 25° E. (Vancouver) to nil (Windsor, Ont.) to 23° W. (Halifax).
India—Nil.

CONVERTING TRUE BEARING.

INTO MAGNETIC AND VICE-VERSA.

To find true if variation is W., subtract the degrees

www.ingramcontent.com/pod-product-compliance
Lightning Source LLC
LaVergne TN
LVHW051347080426
835509LV00020BA/3323